This book is dedicated with love to The Beautiful Wendy.

Grateful thanks for feedback and editing help to Chris McMahon, Jeopardy Champion Dave Meddish, Laura Smith and Sarah Wakefield.

Table of Contents

1. Prelude
2. A Blast from the Past
3. So, This is Madrid
4. Christmas in Vermont
5. Longing
6. Madrid Oddities
7. The Narnia Chapter
8. The Year of Living Dangerously
9. Philosophy
10. A Pig Leg in Paris
11. The Grillmaster
12. Rain, Spaniards, Bullfighting and the Mafia
13. Herding Cats and Riot Day in Berlin
14. Spaniards: The Good, the Bad and the Ugly
15. *Capea* or "How to Eat Dirt and Like It."
16. Wedding in Provence
17. They Love It When You Try
18. Beggars Revisited
19. Deep Cleaning
20. Risky Business in Galicia
21. The Joys of Flying
22. Provence and the Shower From Hell
23. The Burning of the Bulls in Candeleda
24. I was Promised Kittens
25. A Day in the Life
26. Segovia and the Golden Nose
27. Revelation

Prelude

I'm bored. Bored like an immortal who has wandered the entire planet and experienced everything. I feel like I have seen it all, done it all, tasted it all and am absolutely sure there is nothing left here for me.

I don't like to travel and why should I? I have a big screen TV and over a hundred channels that have shown me the wars, the wildlife and the wonders that man or nature has created. Why do I need to go anywhere to see or do anything? I have a supermarket down the road with every taste imaginable and every dish is nothing but a small variation on things I have been eating for over thirty years.

I was bored with life for over a year until my wife of twelve years got ovarian cancer. After that, I spent nine months wishing for a little boredom and then she passed away. I grieved. Now I'm bored again. I run, I go to mixed martial arts classes, I watch a few TV shows, I read, and that's it. I play a few video games, but none of them can hold my attention for longer than half an hour.

I am bored!

Is this all there is to life?

A Blast from the Past

It is August. The phone rings.

"Hello?"

"Jamie!"

"Yes?"

"It's Colette."

I have not heard her voice for over twenty years, yet, I know who it is right away. My eighth grade girlfriend, insanity personified and platinum blond perpetual babe. I know of no other.

"Colette? Wow!"

"Wendy and I are having a barbeque down at the lake house; do you want to come down?"

And then I say the words that Wendy will haunt me with for the rest of my life: "Wendy who?"

"Wendy White."

It takes me three seconds to remember who she is and that leads me to remember the lake house she's talking about. Wendy's dad owns the nicest house in the nicest location on the lake. Wendy was my girlfriend for three weeks when I was eighteen and then her family moved to Pennsylvania and we lost touch.

"I'd love to. I'll be down in half an hour."

I shower, put on what I happen to think at the time are nice clothes (oversized black jeans and a Superman T-shirt) and head down to the lake. I open up the gate to the front lawn and find Colette, Wendy, her father, his girlfriend and a stranger sitting on a blanket. They are all casually shelling pistachios, drinking margaritas and shucking corn. I take one look at Wendy who I have not seen in over twenty years and immediately think "I want that." She is stunning to look at, smiley, effusive, welcoming and the second I see her I am drawn to her like a moth to an inferno.

Colette and Wendy are both five feet five with voluptuous figures and brains that are scary smart. The similarities end there. Colette is Nordic looking, fair skinned, blue eyed and blond. Wendy is dark haired, tanned skin, freckled and eyes of green. She could pass as Spanish or Italian or even Indian but is actually Irish.

We do what people separated for twenty years always do, we tell our stories. I was married for twelve years then my wife died of cancer. I own a nice house in my hometown, have had some success as a writer, and work at the local high school maintaining the computer network.

I know that my stories will pale in comparison to theirs. I am not stupid, but Wendy and Colette are exceptionally smart and strong-willed women. We knew that even in high school. Somehow, we also knew Colette would end up in Paris and Wendy would end up in Spain.

Colette did end up moving to Paris, started her own marketing company and married a Frenchman, Mathieu, the man sitting next to her. Wendy received her law degree, lived in Boston for a few years, then in New York with Colette, worked as a head hunter for a few years and has now started working for Colette's husband, expanding his competitive intelligence agency into Spain, where she now lives.

As the evening progresses, irresistible chemistry pulls Wendy and me together. By the end of the night she is sitting between my legs, wrapped in my arms sitting at the picnic table. I ask her out two days later and we spend the entire day together; and then the next day; and the next. She extends her trip by a week to spend more time with me and also to attend a class reunion. We are inseparable for the entire time she is home. She heads back to Madrid and our international courtship begins, with two or more hours a night on the phone talking.

So, This is Madrid

Now it is October, and I am going to leave North America for the first time in my life to see my beautiful Spanish girlfriend and the city of Madrid.

Keep in mind that I absolutely hate flying. I have a couple shots of Jack Daniels to calm my nerves before boarding my flight to Newark. Of course there is a delay, so we sit on the runway for an hour before finally taking off and by that time, the calming effects of the alcohol have long worn off. There are twenty of us in this tiny plane, and as always there is turbulence. The plane jerks and twitches like Rush Limbaugh doing his exaggerated imitation of Michael J. Fox.

I decided a few years ago that fear was not going to stop me from having adventures and enjoying life to the fullest. I do my best to think of this as an adventure. I try chatting every so often to the doctor seated next to me as he reads some truly gripping articles on intestinal diseases. Despite being scared to death of heights, I force myself to look out the window at the vast forests of both Vermont and New York as we fly over them, doing my best to absorb and appreciate as much of this journey as I can no matter how petrifying.

Thanks to Wendy's planning, I have three hours between flights and arrive with plenty of time to make my connection. Despite arriving ninety minutes late, I still have ninety minutes to make my next flight. I make a quick stop at a bar for a refill on liquid courage and make my way to the gate for my plane which is already boarding.

The plane to Madrid is quite the opposite of the puddle-jumper I just flew into Newark on. It is both enormous and packed. There are no free seats anywhere, the passengers are all tiny and all of them are speaking Spanish. It's a seven hour flight. Luckily, I am able to fall asleep shortly after we leave the ground.

I wake up quite a bit later and grab a stewardess who sits down opposite me when I touch her arm. "Excuse me, how long until we land?"

"About forty minutes."

Oh my God, I am so the winner!

Six hours and twenty minutes of a transatlantic flight have evaporated.

There is no turbulence and we have smooth flying into

Madrid.

I take my time gathering my stuff and am one of the last to leave. I exit the plane and... no one is around. Where the hell are the other passengers? I was right behind them. Even the people behind me have disappeared!

I have a huge maze of hallways leading in every direction in front of me. Right? Left? Straight? Where the hell do I go from here? I start wandering randomly and eventually find what looks like a check-in area: a place for people to board planes. That can't be right- I head back the way I came and look for some sort of luggage pick up area. Airports are confusing for someone who has no idea what they are supposed to be doing or where they are supposed to be going and attempt to do so once every couple decades.

Wendy's probably frantic right now.

I find someone who speaks a bit of English and she points me back to the way I just came. I enter a long line of people who look like they're checking in. I am sure that in ten minutes I'm going to be a thousand feet in the air pleading "No! Wait, I just got here! Let me off!"

As it turns out, this is the immigration and passport control line. I am not hassled and allowed to proceed as normal into the next room.

Hey look! There's my luggage! Woo hoo!!!

I snag my suitcase and start looking for an exit. There's a door, wonder where that leads? Oh look, right into the waiting arms of my beautiful Spanish girl.

"Hey beautiful."

"Hey handsome."

Life is good.

She caresses my face affectionately, smiling with love and asks "How are you doing?"

"I'm fine; a little groggy for some reason. I slept the whole way here but still feel tired." I grab her and pull her close. Her smile is breathtaking. She beams at me like a sun made human female. She hugs me tight, then finally turns away, summons us a cab, we load our stuff into it and off we go. She turns towards me in the seat and focuses her million-watt smile and beautiful green eyes on me. "You're here! You're finally here!"

"I am! I am in Europe, the old country." So far it looks a lot like America with big highways, lots of traffic, graffiti all over the walls and bridges. Wendy notices me appraising things out the window.

"Don't think this is representative of Madrid. Airports are always set way outside the city in barren areas."

"Okay."

We get back to her place and it is five floors up to her apartment with no elevator. She has a beautiful place though with an enormous terrace, white marble floors, two bathrooms and a blue bedroom. We immediately collapse in bed and laugh and talk and play for a couple hours and then she lets me get some sleep while she gets some work done. I wake up at either mid-afternoon, or mid-evening, depending on how you look at it. There is a six hour time differential from Madrid to Vermont.

The day is clear and beautiful and I start to notice the difference in the sun. It hammers you like a physical force here, in a way I am unfamiliar with in my northern state of Vermont. Thank God for parasols. (Do you know that in Spanish "para" means "for" and "sol" means "sun?") Wendy knows what she wants to show me and orders us a pile of raw steak that comes with a steaming, searing cooking surface. It is a stone with bright coals under it and we cook the meat on it right at our table. I order a Coke for a drink. When it comes I take one sip of it; shocked, I pull it away and look at it as if it had bit me. Truth be told, it kind of did.

This Coke tastes like it used to when I was a kid. When I was little, my grandfather always had Coke in the fridge and it was my favorite soda. I liked the bite it had. For a child, it was like whiskey is to an adult. A drink with teeth. As I got older, I knew the taste had changed. Somehow, it had become more syrupy and smooth, losing the bite it once had. That's because they switched from using cane sugar to using corn syrup in America. Yummy! Soda made with corn! This is because America has a powerful corn lobby and a not so powerful cane lobby. A lot more states produce corn. So, there are tariffs on all the cane sugar that comes into America, and we pay twice as much for sugar than any other country in the world.

In Madrid, Coke tastes like Coke is supposed to taste and bites you when you drink it. Just like it is supposed to.

Good stuff.

And now, it is time for my education to begin. Not with facts and figures and museums, but with wide-eyed wonder and awe. We are going sight-seeing.

I have the mistaken belief that the differences between people and places are all minor. Europe is older than America, yeah, I get that. Denmark is more liberal than the United States, I get that too. Parisians are generally fashionable; my countrymen are usually morbidly obese. All pretty minor differences. People are people the world over, and places are places with some different architecture. Big deal. What happens next is days and days of enlightenment.

In order to best experience the city, we walk everywhere. Unfortunately, Madrid is not a flat city. Somehow, everything is uphill. Wendy lives in a little hollow, and if we head north, south or west, we start out walking up steep steps. Only east leads downhill and there is nothing to see east. I now understand how someone can walk "uphill both ways" to school when they were young. We will leave to see a sight, immediately walking up stairs to get to a main street, somehow we will circle around and seven hours later end up walking uphill to get back to her building. I don't even understand how it is possible.

The first thing I notice when we start today's walk is all the bars. Everywhere there are little cafes. Mile after mile of cafes with little lawn chairs and tables with sun umbrellas as far as the eye can see. Spaniards love being outside in the sun sipping a beer and can chat for hours. At every table we pass there are large frosty round glasses of beer for each person.

I quickly learn that things are more relaxed in Madrid culture when compared to America's strict rules and endless regulations. Zoning, for instance. You can put up as many tables and chairs in front of your restaurant as you want as long as pedestrians can get through the sidewalk. Because of this, all the cafes have as many tables and chairs out in front of them as will fit in the sun.

Wendy explains that on a sunny day in Madrid, which is most days, the places are always just shy of full. There are usually a couple free seats outside, a couple free inside, or a short wait. It's like the entire country has an organized plan that establishments will only fill up to ninety percent and then the next group goes somewhere else. In Madrid, they love their gatherings, and there's always room for more!

The architecture is nothing like what I expected. As a man who has always been enamored of myths, heroism and fantasy, this city is a visual gold mine. Every step we take a new, huge display of men in full armor on horses comes into a view or possibly a fountain with Poseidon being pulled by sea horses. Around the next corner is an army of valkyries on a rooftop. We pass a building with a golden domed roof and a naked ebony angel standing on top, arms and wings outspread. There are endless fountains populated by mermaids. There are statues of men in chariots charging into war, enormous marble lions and giants holding up buildings. It's hard for me to fathom why Madrid is such a wonder for me every place we go. It's not that I don't understand why I love it so much, it's that I don't understand why it's designed this way. I knew Europe was the old country, but I had no idea that meant that everywhere you go looks like a scene from a Tolkien or C. S. Lewis book.

What's even more amazing is that these aren't super special buildings or places. One display that must have taken up an acre in front a building was so breathtaking I asked Wendy "What's in that fantastic building with the flowers and the fountain and the statues out front?

"The post office."

And it is then that I come to the conclusion that I understand nothing. That I am not an immortal who has seen and done everything nor is it possible to do so from my big screen TV. It is a question of scale.

The scale of everything I've mentioned is enormous. We're not talking little statues for kids to climb on. We're talking pillars that rise into the sky like they belong in Olympus. This is something I never realized while sitting in front of my TV. We see things that would look boring on TV, but up close they awe you with their size and grandeur. You can't fathom the difference between seeing a statue a hundred and twenty-five feet high on your TV versus actually standing under it. Or backing up so far to try and get a picture and finding you have to keep backing up further and further and further before you can get the whole thing to fit in the camera lens.

She takes me to Retiro Park and the Thyssen museum. Wendy has very few plans to take me to museums but a little culture never hurts. The Thyssen was suggested to me by my friend Peter Jensen since he loves it when he visits Madrid. It's impressive but as is the style of the time, the paintings are always of royalty or scenes from the Bible; neither of which hold our attention very long. We stroll through and take a look at things that catch our eyes and then decide we're not really museum people and make our way over to Retiro Park.

Madrid is one of the greenest cities in Europe and the Retiro is a perfect example of this. There are acres of space for picnics, nature walks, beautiful rose gardens, sculptured trees, a man-made lake teeming with koi, boats you can rent, an all glass building with an art display inside and enough massive statues to make Middle Earth look mundane. Across the artificial lake is an intricate, towering statue that must be fifty meters high. At the top is King Alfonso XII on a horse. The horse is standing on a casket. Then upon a platform supported by Roman style pillars, a gathering of angels gesturing and holding each other, one of them with a book in her hand. Beneath that a mosaic carved in black marble. That's only one side. There is a different scene on the four walls beneath the platform. Surrounding all of this are statues of Aslan-sized lions, mermaids and fish.

Elsewhere, there are multiple ponds with ducks and geese in them. One of the few statues in the world that actually depicts Lucifer's fall from heaven. There are palm readers, street performers and of course, cafes with little tables out for beer drinking and people-watching. We wander for a bit and marvel at how many people have blankets and bottles of wine and picnic baskets basking in the sun without it ever seeming the least bit crowded. We feed the koi, take a look at the bizarre art inside the glass building and feed the geese in a pond.

Now we're hot and it's time to do one of our favorite things: have a beer, people watch and chat. We do that for an hour under a canopy at a nice bar overlooking the man-made pond with a nice sidewalk in front of it that provides a view of lots of families walking by and teenagers looking to hook up. As Will Smith says in his song "Summertime"- "Guys out hunting and girls doing likewise." A short walk away is our next stop.

Wendy wants to take me to the Reina Sofía Museum to see *Guernica;* a painting by Pablo Picasso. It is inspired by Picasso's horror at the Nazi German bombing of Guernica, Spain on April 26,

1937 during the Spanish Civil War. It's an overwhelming piece. For one thing, it's gigantic, and there are images within images throughout the painting, all of them depicting the senseless horrors of war. It shows images of the soldiers, but also a woman in pain and a screaming horse rearing, eyes wild.

When viewing the painting for the first time, a German soldier asked Picasso if he was responsible for the painting. To which he replied "No. You are."

I don't like Picasso's work generally but this one is fantastic, frightening, and moving. I think it perfectly symbolizes the violence and tragedy of war that people can sometimes forget.

A copy of the painting hangs in the United Nations building in New York. Perhaps it hangs there as a reminder that nations should think before attacking each other? However, a large curtain was hung over the picture when Colin Powell and John Negroponte gave press conferences at the United Nations urging war against Iraq.

On a lighter note, we leave the gallery and Wendy tells me two of her friends said we should check out a store, "Mundo Fantastico," right near the museum and see what we think. We walk for a bit but don't know where it is. We stop into a little convenience store and Wendy asks for directions. Right next to us is an attractive girl buying a small package of donuts.

"I can take you. I'm going into work there right now."

"Oh, thank you. What do you do there?"

"I'm a stripper."

Okay then!

We follow her into the largest adult complex I have ever seen. I convince Wendy that as a writer it is my duty to explore this place so I can report it to you, faithful reader. I do it all for you. Honest. We walk around for a few minutes and they have tons of everything. It's like the Mall of America for porn. There are toys, videos, dolls, a bar with stripper poles and of course, strippers. There is a live sex show running in a few hours. There are peep booths. All of it meticulously designed and there is not a speck of dirt anywhere. It is two floors of a clean, tastefully designed, almost sterilized store - built for sex. We don't go into every room exploring of course, but we can see the posters outside each area advertising what is inside.

Wendy starts grabbing stuff off the racks until her arms are full.

Horrified I raise my voice to her. "You put that back young lady! I am a good Christian and don't truck with that nonsense!"

She pouts and stamps her foot.

I storm out.

Yeah; that happened...

Dear Wendy's Dad,

The above is a total fiction. Your daughter was a perfect angel the entire time I was there and I understand her wanting to save herself for marriage. I slept on the couch the entire time I was visiting her.

Honorably yours,
Jamie

I think the most fictional part of that story would be Wendy pouting and stamping her foot. No matter how hard I try, I can't even summon up a mental image of that.

We walk around for ten minutes being alternately horrified, fascinated, amused and curious before leaving. Not wanting to be seen as prudes, we buy a couple things.

"Well, that was interesting."

"Yup."

We have gone from the horrors of war to sanitized porn in a very short walk.

It is a fascinating start to my days in Madrid.

The next day I arise late and Wendy works in the morning again.

Wendy has to catch up on some work before tonight's bullfight so I read on the terrace about Spain and the country's amazing leader.

Until 1975 Spain was ruled by a fascist dictator named Francisco Franco. In 1936 Spain democratically elected the "Popular Front" political party into power. A series of events culminated in the right wing, conservative Franco leading a coup against the elected party and Franco seized power and held it with an iron fist until his death in 1975.

Spain now has a king. King Juan Carlos.

Personally groomed by Franco to continue his ultra-conservative agenda, Juan Carlos went in the opposite direction, moving the country more towards democracy every year. Needless to say this upset many of the more conservative political leaders of Spain.

On the night of February 23, 1981 Colonel Tejero launched an attempted coup, bursting into parliament as it was in full session and holding it hostage until his demands were met. That was the plan anyway.

Juan Carlos simply defied his demands and on television ordered all the men back to their barracks. The coup was over in mere hours and the King's popularity soared. In 2005, independent polls showed a positive approval rating for the king by over 75% of the population.

Now that's a leader. I can't tell you how impressed I am with this man. He took a struggling dictatorship and dragged Spain into stability, democracy and the twenty-first century through wisdom and courage.

The part that really matters to me though is the fact that he never puts himself above anyone. Rather than remain a dictator, he introduced democracy. When he goes to the bullfights he doesn't sit in the regal King's box, but instead, close to the action, in the stands, with everyone else.

One night while the King was out riding his motorcycle, a motorist was stranded by the side of the road. Juan Carlos stopped to see what the problem was and found out the man was out of gas. He told him to hop on and took him to get gas and then back to his car. The man asked him his name and to remove his helmet so that he could thank him properly. At first the King refused, not wanting to draw attention to himself, but after repeated requests he eventually relented and took off his helmet. "My name is Juan Carlos."

"Yeah, the King gave me a ride on his motorcycle to get gas. It was cool. We're buds now."

As I type this, George Bush is president. A man who was democratically elected but acts like a dictator above the law.

Reading about Juan Carlos fills me with envy for Spain's leadership.

It is time to get ready for the bullfight.

Let me explain the thoughts I have going into my first bullfight.

Quite a lot of what you view in the world can be tempered by your attitude. Take the sport of mixed martial arts (generally known by its largest promoter, the UFC a.k.a. Ultimate Fighting) for instance. Uneducated and unaware, people will watch a match and just see two guys beating the shit out of each other in a cage. There's blood, there's violence, there's one guy getting the crap pounded out of him or even being choked unconscious. But if you understand what is going on, you can see that it is as cerebral as a chess match. You can see the maneuvering for position. You are aware of one fighter's attempts to pass guard and why that is good but also risky. You understand when someone leaves themselves open and is in danger of being caught if only their opponent sees it as well and knows how to capitalize on that particular opening. You can catch the denial of the arm bar that would end the fight. You can see the specialties of the fighters. You understand the mixture of American wrestling, muay Thai, boxing, Brazilian jiu jitsu, karate and even sumo. You can see what discipline each fighter needs to work on and how well they blend their styles.

This is how I approach bullfighting. Teach me. Educate me. Show me why this is not a brutal slaughter of a defenseless cow and make me understand.

Honestly, I am a little nervous about how I will react to what I am about to see. I would like to think that I have an open mind and I think I have a few advantages the normal viewer might not have in order to appreciate what Spaniards consider an art. I have loved all animals since I was very young and I am fascinated by all wildlife. I have spent thousands of hours watching the Discovery channel because of this love of animals. In doing so, you cannot escape the joy and wonder that is nature nor can you escape the reality that is life and death in the wild. Things die in order for other things to survive. And sometimes, it is not pretty. It is just real.

I have seen a lion chewing on the flank of a downed antelope that is not even dead yet. I have seen a crocodile pull a zebra under the water by one hind leg, the zebra screaming and struggling the entire time, desperate not to go quietly into that good night. I also come from a family of hunters. I have killed a deer and watched it die. It is not fun watching something die, but I think it is necessary if you eat meat. You get an education from viewing these things. You know that in nature and in life, there is death. And death is never pretty. It does not come shrink-wrapped, bloodless, weighed, and labeled for you to take home, unwrap and never have to think about the life that was lost to bring you that meal.

That is how my mind is approaching bullfighting. I know there will be death. It will not be pretty. I am uneducated and looking to be enlightened, with the same attitude I hope others take when I try to enlighten them about the beauty I find in mixed martial arts. Today, Wendy and twenty thousand screaming Spaniards will find beauty in the bullring. I may join them or I may just be horrified. But I'll keep an open mind about it.

Most people bring a *bota* or wineskin of red wine, a white napkin or handkerchief, and a snack, preferably Spain's national food of pride: *jamon*. Jamon will be introduced to me later so today we just have the bota and some white napkins.

Awake and refreshed I notice new things about the city as we walk toward the subway. Coming from a small town, I have always hated American cities. Madrid is different. For one thing, it wasn't designed. It wasn't planned out like modern American cities. It has been a settlement since before man started writing, became more of a town under the Romans, but really started to grow in size in the ninth century. Therefore, in the section we are in, there are no four lane highways with underpasses and exit ramps. There are cobblestone streets with buildings and statues hundreds upon hundreds of years old. The streets and sidewalks are narrow and ancient and quaint. As we walk, I get the feeling of many communities strung together, grown larger as time progresses more than one large city designed from the ground up for millions of people.

I am forty years old and I have never been on a subway. Luckily, Madrid's is very clean, modern and well maintained. Have I mentioned I hate people? And crowds? And noise? And flying? Because I do. A lot.

I had a massive panic attack at work one day and it took me years to recover. Now I avoid all of the above like the plague. With a couple years of therapy and medication I regained a semblance of normalcy but the medication had added thirty plus pounds to my frame and made the world muted and dull. I eventually decided to go off the medication and try to manage my anxiety problems through exercise, proper diet and the occasional visit to my Doctor: the esteemed Doctor Jack Daniels.

We climb onto the subway and, voila, it is packed to bursting, mostly with people on their way to the bullring. I hold Wendy close to me with one arm and grab an overhanging bar with my other. We sway in time with the motion of the train and my muscles flex enough to try and make the ride smooth as she snuggles against me for nine stops.

"I'm sorry about this. Are you okay?"

Wendy knows about my "issues." I smile and mean it. "Just fine darling; just fine. No worries at all."

The outside of the bullring is enormous and clearly influenced by Muslim architecture with many arcs and designs without depictions of men or animals. Outside the bullring is a chaos of vendors selling snacks, T-shirts, water and beer, scalpers and patrons are milling about waiting for people or just talking and drinking. There is barely room to maneuver to the door. We go inside, rent some cushions for a Euro each and grab our "seats." It is just as you would imagine it if you had lived two thousand years ago. Ascending stone seats in a massive circular coliseum, people wedged in like sardines to make the best use of all available space. Unlike America, there is no advertising. There are no banners flying above the ring, no beer or sports advertisements on the walls inside the ring. This is art, not sport, to Spaniards. We elbow our way to our assigned seats, settle down on our cushions, adjust elbows and knees with our very close neighbors and I take a pull off the bota.

Every seat is taken. Twenty thousand screaming Spaniards surround me and I don't speak the language. How am I able to deal with this? For some reason, Wendy seems to have the ability to expand my boundaries without fear. For her, I will fly, visit a city, ride on a full to bursting subway car, sit with thousands of tightly packed people, and somehow, completely against my history, *not* freak out.

It is time to begin.

A bull is let into the ring through a small passage and is blinded by the sunshine and surprised by the sudden noise of the crowd. He charges the first man he sees. The man quickly runs behind a narrow barrier. Another man emerges, further away and waves a cape and the bull charges him. He also dashes behind a barrier too narrow for the bull to follow.

Wendy saw her first bullfight at fifteen when she lived in Madrid for a year with her mother so she starts to explain to me what I am seeing, the stages of the bullfight. What the picador does. Who the minions are and which one is the matador. Why the crowd is screaming *"Muy mal! Muy mal!"* (Very bad!) at certain bulls or even at the matadors.

I am fascinated by it for the same reason I am fascinated by the UFC. It is a man testing himself against a twelve hundred pound animal. And in case you didn't know, they do get gored.

Sometimes they survive.

And sometimes they do not.

Without the element of mortal danger, bullfighting would hold no appeal to me.

Wendy explains to me that this is not a fair fight nor is it meant to be. The bull is going to die except in very rare cases, possibly one in a thousand, where the bull is so valiant he is pardoned and spends the rest of his life breeding fine looking cows. Usually, the bulls are going to die. I accept that. Just as I accept that bulls die every day in America. They usually die after a life in a factory farm with a nail through the head, herded in a line, terrified of the smell of death and terror of the other cows. For them, there is no chance to gore someone, no chance to fight, just methodically killed.

The fighting bulls of Spain lead a free-range, wonderful life on fantastically lush ranches until their day in the ring. I know if I was a bull, I'd choose free range over factory and the fight over the nail.

The crowd evaluates everything in a bullfight. They examine when a matador is being cowardly or when the bull is damaged in some way and needs to be replaced. They can see a lame left leg that neither Wendy nor I can pick up. They can see when a matador is pretending to do something dangerous and in reality, it is not dangerous at all. The moves are interesting for the rubes like me, but the season ticket holders are happy to explain to Wendy what we are really seeing.

The first bullfighter, Luis Francisco Esplá, is close to fifty years old. He is the senior of course, and it is clear that he is a master of his craft. He is in no danger. Wendy explains that later in the night, if one of the other fighters gets gored, it will be his responsibility to come out and finish the bull. A bull who now understands it is not the cape he needs to attack for results. He is impressive in his skill and understanding, but the element of danger is lacking. It's like watching Mike Tyson fight Pee Wee Herman.

The next two that come out are much younger. They are in their early twenties. Wendy is afraid; sits very close to me and holds one of my hands in hers and with the other clenches and unclenches her hand on my bicep throughout the fights. She warns me that the young matadors are filled with bluster and bravado, assured of their own immortality. They are the ones who will take the risk and get gored by being careless.

Okay, now I'm interested.

It becomes immediately clear she is right, but still hard to imagine one of them being caught. The bulls love the cape and attack it with dogged persistence. Wendy explains that the bulls will do this for fifteen minutes then they will start to understand that the cape is not the enemy, and that's when the real danger starts.

Wendy is explaining things to me as the bulls come out one by one to face their opponent, their killer, and next to her, a season ticket holder will lean over and explain to her some minute point she has missed. He is a fountain of knowledge that she taps randomly throughout the next ninety minutes.

"Why is the crowd asking to have the bull replaced?"

"He has a lame left leg."

We can't see it.

"Why is the crowd screaming to the matador "Muy mal!"?

"That was supposed to be a killing blow and he missed. The sword has fallen out. He will have to try it again."

He fails again and the crowd goes ballistic with shouts, whistles and protest clapping. Despite outsider perception, the bull is not supposed to suffer. The bull is supposed to be killed humanely, with dignity and as little cruelty as possible and when a bullfighter lacks the skill to do this adequately, the crowd voices their displeasure.

It is interesting. I am not horrified or enraptured. I start to become more fascinated the more I understand, but still I miss the danger. The matadors are too good, and this should be a contest not a show. There should be real risk and real danger, or why even bother?

There are six bulls. There are three matadors who each come out and do one bull each, a very short two minute intermission, and then three more bulls for the matadors.

The sixth bull shows promise.

This bull is filled with spirit. The crowd cheers him. They like his style and he is not a coward. This could be a good fight. A twenty-three year old matador, Miguel Angel Perera, comes out to fight him. Swagger and bravado and machismo suffuse his being as he comes to face this fourteen hundred pound (six hundred kilos) animal that has never seen a man alone, on foot, and facing him.

The bull charges fiercely. The man's feet do not move as an animal akin to a freight train bears down on him. He is standing with his left side to the bull, looking over his shoulder, but his body is not facing him. My imagination is filled with images of this slight man being smashed in the hips, spine shattered as he goes over the bull's head. Moments before the bull reaches him, he casually waves the cape *behind* his back. Try to imagine that for just a second. Not a flag waving in front of him with the full reach of his arm to protect him, and sight to warn him if the bull is veering off course. No, he waves the flag behind him, and over a thousand pounds of bone, muscle, horns and aggression go flying past his ass, his spine and his bowels. The man's feet have not moved. He has not adjusted one iota for the charge. The bull spins around, furious, to face him for another charge and Perera throws his hands to his sides, puffs out his chest, raises up on his toes and thrusts his groin at the bull in challenge and showmanship.

The crowd deafens me with their cheers.

It is all about the passes. He does a few more graceful but dangerous passes and you can sense the bull thinking, reasoning. He is clearly trying to get the measure of this infuriating target. How come he keeps missing? How come his deadly horns keep hitting air? This has never happened before.

The bull finally catches the bullfighter's leg and hurls him high into the air. He lands on the ground flat and hard. The minions are quick and distract the bull immediately from the matador on the ground and Perera stands and limps over to his cape. He has been hit and his leg is now bleeding. He is cut and most certainly bruised in multiple places. The crowd makes appropriate worried noises. His minions try to pick him up and carry him to go to the infirmary but he refuses, shaking their hands off him. They tie a tourniquet around his upper leg to slow the bleeding. I grab Wendy's hand tightly. As a long-time bullfighting aficionado, she has seen matadors get badly gored, worse than this, but this fight is getting harder and harder for her to watch.

Despite his injury, Perera continues to work his bull, powering through the danger and pain. He is determined to win the crowd as he forces the bull to charge him again and again in tighter and tighter circles. He is unafraid. To me, at this moment, he is courage incarnate. The bull has hit him once which means the bull is gaining his measure. He is learning where the man is. Time marches on and Perera, leaking blood, refuses to stop doing closer and closer passes. The crowd is cheering and clapping at his every move.

Finally the bull is exhausted. His labored breathing is visible even from the stands. His stomach is rising and falling like a long distance runner's. Perera stands right in front of him. Not right in front of him, as in, in a straight line. Right in front of him like a lover. Right in front of him like an angry drunk spoiling for a fight; face to snout. He waves the cape behind his back. "Come mister bull; come right through me to get to your hated adversary. I know you are tired, but it is right here. It is right behind this man. Come for it." The cape dangles out of reach and if the bull lifts his head swiftly, he will impale the man and lift him off his feet and the man will die.

The matador stares him down and the bull stands there, exhausted.

The bell sounds, signaling that fifteen minutes are up. We have entered the most dangerous part of the fight since at this duration the average bull is beginning to understand the difference between cape and man. Most fights are done by now. To continue is folly. And this bull has caught him once. It is staggering that he is continuing.

I am breathless. So is the rest of the crowd. Wendy glances again at the program. She leans over to me, "Last year, he was gored badly in this ring. He had to take the rest of the season off it was so bad."

I stare at her aghast. "Are you kidding me? He was gored in this ring and he continues to challenge this bull long after the fifteen minutes bell has sounded?"

He taunts the bull with the cape some more, provoking it to charge him again and again. The bull passes two more times and stops. Exhausted, the bull stares at him. Inches from the bull, he stares back.

He turns his back on the bull, showing his lack of fear and mastery. He does not even glance over his shoulder at the bull to make sure of his own safety. He just turns his back, and walks slowly away, the cape hanging low at his side. He walks over to the railing and a minion hands him the killing sword.

He calmly walks back out into the center of the ring with the killing sword. Now that the bull has rested a moment, he has more energy. Perera takes up a position, sword leveled with his eyes as if sighting a rifle. He shakes the cape at the bull again and the bull charges. Perera runs *at the bull,* leaps into the air, sword extended, delivering a killing thrust to the back and down into the heart, then twists his body away from the horns, away from the rising head looking to impale him. He nimbly steps away from the bull. The bull staggers. The bull is five feet from him, wounded, enraged, and still alive. Perera is oblivious; confident. He turns his back on the bull and raises his hands.

The bull falls on its side.

The crowd rises as one, furiously waving their white handkerchiefs, demanding he be rewarded. We are with them. Shaking our white handkerchiefs like salt over steak and cheering until we are raw. Such skill! Such courage after being gored in this very ring only a year before!

Unbelievable!

The president grants him two ears and he is carried out of the *puerte grande* on the shoulders of his minions. People rip off parts of his clothes as souvenirs as he is carried out.

The crowd empties quickly. It is dark. As per tradition of Wendy and her circle of friends we head up to "Los Timbales" also known simple as "The Bull Bar." It is packed with people from the bullring. Wendy snakes her way through the crowd to the bar while I look for a place to put drinks, finally finding a windowsill outside. There are so many people here that the bar is surrounded by the crowd that is spilling into the street. We are lucky to even have a windowsill to place tapas and drinks. I am in awe of what I have seen and Wendy is thrilled. We have a couple of glasses of wine, some tapas and then it is time to head home.

Today is more viewing of what makes Madrid uniquely Madrid. We need a few things for tomorrow's barbeque so Wendy takes me to an indoor market with dozens of rented stalls each about the size of a small store. One of them has a little bit of everything, really just a small convenience store for people who don't want to head to the supermarket for milk or eggs. Many sell nothing but fruits and vegetables. There are a couple bars and a lot of seafood stands.

I am drawn to the sea in a variety of ways. I live for the coast. I will walk in the ocean, chest high, for hours; outstretched hands feeling the water flow through my fingers and over my arms while observing all the people on the beach. I will run for miles on the sand. I love visiting large, well maintained aquariums and watching the fish for hours. And oddly, I am drawn to anyplace with fish on display. Live lobster and crab tanks, fish stacked high, piles of shrimp or clams or scallops all on ice. I am drawn to them and have to see what is for sale when I pass any seafood stand.

I eat a lot of fish and seafood. I've always liked all kinds of the sea's bounty, but since I've changed my diet (in order to drop forty pounds of middle-aged fat) I eat fish three or even four times a week. They know me by name at the local Hannaford seafood section.

As we wander and I continue to stop at every stall, Wendy is explaining to me about how big a percentage fish and seafood is in the diet of Spain. I cannot fathom how much seafood is in this place. Of the dozen or so stands here, each one is as big, if not bigger than the entire seafood section of Hannaford's, which is enormous. And the fish and seafood are packed six inches high in each of the stands. There are about three dozen varieties of fish of all sizes, all with the head on, various kinds of shrimp, mussels, squid, octopus, barnacles and best of all, four different kinds of lobster. Four! One kind of lobster I saw, I initially thought was a hybrid. It had a shrimp's body with long, thin lobster claws on it. Wendy tells me the sign says it is "Cigala" but she doesn't know what that is either. After we do some research we find out that it is commonly known in English as a "Norwegian Lobster."

It looks like a huge shrimp with long, slender lobster claws. I am determined that someday, I will learn how to prepare those and make them into a meal for Wendy and me. As well as those lobsters, they had the typical lobster we usually get in Maine, the spiny clawless ones that you get around Florida, and a white lobster like nothing I have ever seen before.

(A little research later informs me that American Lobster color mutations are rare but exist. The white one I saw was not a different species of lobster, but was special in its own way, being the rarest color of that species of lobster ever found. There are four colors of American Lobster. There are the normal greenish-brown lobsters, and there are brilliant, azure blue lobsters which are the most common of the rare colors. Approximately one in every two million lobsters is blue. There are also pale yellow lobsters that have been caught; the chances on those being one in thirty million. The last and most rare lobster is the albino or "crystal" lobster which is seen once out of every *one hundred million* lobsters! And I saw one!)

Then we are off to the site of the 2003 bombings, the Atocha Train Station. It is an incredibly well-designed, modern, shiny building filled with ticket counters, car rental places, coffee shops, bars and an amazing restaurant that overlooks the jungle. Yes, the jungle. We turn one corner and imagine my surprise when we get inside and there is a forest in the middle of the building about twenty yards on a side and a hundred yards long. There are exotic plants, birds, trees arcing up thirty feet in the air and at one end, an extensive turtle pond with hundreds of turtles in it.

What kind of monster would bomb turtles?

We get a couple of beers at one of the bars situated close by and watch turtles for a while. Life is good and I again have the feeling I have seen nothing of this world. I am enjoying the turtle and people-watching and can't get over my wonder at this jungle in the middle of a train station. I crave another beer. And more time here. Luckily, I'm picking up Spanish at an alarming rate, which is completely surprising to me considering I failed two years of it in high school.

For example -
"Want another beer Wendy?"
"Sure"
I go to the counter.
"Dos cervezas por favor."
"Grande?"
"Si."

He pours me two huge beers.
"Gracias."

We walk home and I see more amazing architecture and some awful fashion. Mullets are huge in Madrid right now. Every now and then, as we walk, Wendy will grab my arm, press against me and whisper "Oh my God, that is so awful" and three guys will walk by with a haircut from the eighties, looking like old country rock stars.

Tonight is Spanish specialty food night. There is a beautiful restaurant just across the street that specializes in paella. We head over at eight forty-five, but they're not even open yet. Everything happens later in Madrid. Nine in the evening is socially the same as four in the afternoon in the states. Restaurants are just barely opening for dinner. We head back across the street to a new little tavern that has just opened and get a glass of wine to sip while we wait. It is a charming little place and, as usual, they love Wendy. I'm not sure if the Spanish people are friendlier to strangers than in America or if it's just the fact she's stunning and wants to give them money. But everywhere we go, they love her. I am a little tired from all our walking today and get a Red Bull while Wendy gets a Rioja red wine. Some olive tapas come, but I don't have any as I am saving my appetite for paella.

We chat with the locals for a bit, one of them doing his best to speak in English and assure me that he's not hitting on Wendy, it's just the way he is. That's right you huge muscle-bound bald guy, you fear the forty-one-year-old, out of shape, King of the Fatties. The bar is very jovial and a nice half hour excursion into a place Wendy wanted to explore anyway.

We head back across the street and the restaurant is open. Since it's so very, very early in Madrid, we're the only ones in the place the entire time we eat. We feel very touristy and a little stupid, but, man, it's not only after nine, but my body clock says it's after three a.m. and I haven't had dinner yet!

We order some seafood paella and some oyster mushrooms as an appetizer. The mushrooms are delicious. Large flat things like I have never seen soaked in olive oil (like everything in Madrid) with tiny bits of chopped *jamon* on them.

The paella arrives a short time later and looks delicious. I love rice. I love seafood. How can this not be fantastic? "Fast food" hasn't taken off in Spain and paella is a perfect example of this. The shrimp, cigala, and mussels are still in their shells decorating the top of the rice which is a golden yellow color from saffron; the most expensive spice in the world. Mixed into the rice are pieces of fish, green and red peppers, calamari, sepia and green peas. We alternate between big spoonfuls of rice and peeling things out of their shells to pop into our mouth while sipping a fine white wine.

It has been a great day and I have experienced a new taste in saffron. We collapse into bed in a heap; the long day of walking combined with new experiences and tastes has left me fatigued. My final thought before being consumed by exhaustion is that, sadly, my first visit is dwindling to a close in Madrid.

Wendy and I get up and it is barbeque day. Almost all of her friends are coming over that evening to meet me and we have work to do. No one lives above Wendy, so she has the entire stairway leading up to the top floor apartment to store her extra patio stuff. Extra chairs, leaves for the table, cushions for the couch and other things are stacked neatly. All of those have to come down and be arranged and then Lena and Stefan are coming over to light the grill, make mojitos and help us get ready.

We get that mostly done and Wendy jumps in the shower. I go lie down on the couch and read some chapters in Steve Savage's book, but then rest my eyes for just a minute and fall asleep for what seems like mere moments. Wendy wakes me up and tells me I was asleep for two hours. Jet lag is evil.

Lena and Stefan show up before everyone else and Lena is charged with making mojitos and Stefan is charged with being the grill-master. I have never had a mojito so I watch Lena make up a couple that I will bring out for Stefan and me to sip while we make fire. Because that's what men do: make fire.

The drink is finally finished and it looks like something a child would make. It is a pale white liquid full of leaves and water, the liquid equivalent of a mud pie. But, as usual, I am surprised and enlightened by the taste which is both ethereal and over-powering. Wendy and Lena watch my stunned reaction, waiting for a response.

"It's like drinking an old growth forest" I exclaim in wonder. Pause. "Wait, that's not quite right. It gives me the feeling of drinking something elvish, in the middle of an old growth forest. It tastes like something Tolkien would invent and have one of his elves serve in a moss-encrusted ancient city."

I bring one out to the terrace for Stefan. He and I sip mojitos and chat while he tends the charcoal which is stubbornly resisting his efforts. I try to help once and he comically waves me off "Don't do that. Don't do that. Don't mess with the Grill-master!" So I just sit and chat with him. I'm no grill-master; I use gas so I'll let him handle it. He looks more like a smoke-master to me. Wendy and Lena are flitting about the apartment getting ready for the party while I wonder how I got here, sip a drink that tastes like it sprang from a fantasy novel and reminisce about the amazing sights I have seen and the new tastes I have experienced in my short time here.

I have been so blind.

More and more people start to show up and the grilling begins as well as introductions all around. The party is amazing. Wendy's friends welcome me with open arms and luckily, all speak English. Many of them have read my website and ask me questions about Magic, UFC, writing, how I like Madrid, bullfights and the party. Without a single exception, I find all of them fascinating, kind and interesting to talk to. I am filled with the feeling that I could really fit in here and enjoy the company of all of them if the future works out the way I think it will. Considering I'm not all that good with parties, it's a great relief to me. Because, you know, when you're in love with a beautiful girl living in Madrid, it seems kind of important that you like her friends, and they like you. As with most Madrid parties, it lasts until well into the morning.

We sleep until after one in the afternoon the next day and then start getting ready for another bullfight. I fill a bota, Wendy grabs our tickets off the fridge and we're off to the bullring. There is a saying in Spain – "If there are bulls there are no bullfighters. If there are bullfighters, then there are no bulls."

Today, neither decided to show up. It looked like clowns chasing frightened cows around the ring. We both need a stiff drink after that, and, as traditional, head up-street to the bull bar "Los Timbales."

Wendy tells me a Spanish joke that perfectly describes the event.

"Juan, you look ecstatic, where are you going?"

"The bullfights!"
"Excellent! Have fun!"
Later that day.
"Juan, you look so sad. Where are you coming from?"
"Sigh. The bullfights."

We are now at the bar sipping a fine Rioja red wine. "I am so happy you got to see a good bullfight as your first."

"Me too! It instilled a love of it in me that is something I think we will share for years. If I had seen that last performance as my first bullfight I would never want to see another, as well as wonder if there was something wrong with you I wasn't aware of."

We order some *"Rabo de Toro"* which is actually bull tail stew. It tastes a lot like pot roast with thick gravy and boiled potatoes. It becomes one of my favorite meals in Madrid.

I wipe some gravy off my chin and throw the napkin on the floor. It's not my fault; it's the custom. Trash cans are to be aimed for, not hit. In every little restaurant or pub we have been into there are little one foot high trash cans around the entire place. Surrounding the trash cans are shrimp peelings, napkins, and other little pieces of refuse. The first place Wendy took me to I noticed this, as it was a place that specialized in shrimp, and around each little bar stand was a pile of shrimp peelings. People throw napkins at the trash cans and if they hit, they hit, if not they stay on the floor. Every now and then someone comes around and sweeps everything up and the cycle repeats.

It is explained to me that a bar with no napkins or other trash on the floor must be devoid of customers and not very good. Which begs the question: why don't they sweep up the trash when it's busy and put it in a bag, then open in the morning and empty the bag on the floor?

Today we are again going to the bullfights, this time with friends. I met a fascinating American barbeque night and, after about five minutes chatting, I was already intrigued thinking about what could happen to him while he was in Madrid. For one thing, he's muscular, and most Spanish men are very slender. For another, he is bald, and is a test driver for an American auto company, so, he's quite

31

interesting to talk to and ask questions about his work. For another, he's very charismatic, and there was at least one woman at the party who was very interested in him. He's going to have a good time in Madrid.

The man's name is Derek, and he's over here visiting Wendy's friend, Candy. He and Candy have been friends for fifteen years. Today is Derek's first bullfight. When you're in Madrid, you have to see a bullfight. It's a rule. True story. They ask you at the airport, before you board a plane:

1. Did a dark mysterious stranger offer to pack your bags?
2. Do you have any animals or fruit stuffed down your pants?
3. How did you like the bullfights?

If you don't have a good answer ready for question number three, you're removed from the line, regarded with suspicion and certainly not allowed to board the plane.

So, we have to meet up with them, and Wendy and I are going to try to explain what's going on in the ring to Derek, because, well, I have become a bit of an aficionado now, thanks to Wendy. We all meet up at a subway stop, and then get out at the bull ring, and the line is hundreds of people long. It's like a rock concert. Two lines extend from the entrance of the bullfight, all the way out to the street, and then split, and head in opposite directions down the sidewalk a hundred people deep waiting to get in.

It takes about an hour to get our tickets, and we get some good ones. We paid thirty-five Euros for them and they were well worth it. We have great seats, right above where the bulls come charging into the ring.

Oddly, we can't quite grasp where all the people went. Despite two lines, a hundred yards long apiece, the arena looks empty today. Of course, it does hold twenty-two thousand people so if ten thousand people show up and stand in line, the inside can still be less than half full. It is quite a change from the last time we were here when every seat was packed right up to the nosebleed seats. Behind us is a small group of Asian tourists. They left after the third bull.

Remember the Spanish saying – "If there are bulls there are no bullfighters. If there are bullfighters, then there are no bulls." Today, with Derek and Candy, the bulls decided to show up.

Wendy is sitting next to Derek so that she can explain to him what's going on, and I lean over every now and then to interject my own little tidbits I've learned. Like me, he has an open mind and is interested to see what it's all about and then decide to be horrified or become a fan.

The first bull that comes out is a disaster. The most cowardly bull we have ever seen. Some people start to protest, and I wonder why the president does not have him removed, which is part of his responsibility. Wendy explains that a bull cannot be replaced because of cowardice. A bull can only be replaced due to an injury, like a lame leg.

Because of this bull being so different from the usual Spanish Fighting Bull, born and bred to battle anything with courage and determination, the first bull fight is a travesty. I've seen seven Matadors take on thirteen bulls so far and this one leaves a bad taste in my mouth. It is a taste like "wow, the critics are right, this is a horribly cruel sport." This bull was unlike any of the others we had seen. He wasn't interested in charging or fighting or goring at all. It was like the Matador was thrown into the ring with a cuddly panda. And we had to watch him kill it, slowly, over the course of fifteen agonizing minutes.

The second bull comes roaring into the ring like a freight train looking to roll over anything that moves. He has aggression and charges easily. Derek gets his first view of what a bullfight is supposed to look like.

The next bull into the ring is even more aggressive than the last, and is colored white. He charges full bore at the first minion, and the minion quickly jumps over the side wall. The bull smashes into the wall at a 45 degree angle, and breaks off a horn! Then he charges another minion and when the minion hides he leaps over the wall into the second circle of the bull ring, where people and staff usually go to escape or wait to clean up the ring after every fight.

This causes a lot of things to happen very rapidly.

Dozens of people on that side of the wall immediately start to bail over the side, into the bull ring. Wendy jumps out of her seat, jumps behind me, grabs my shoulders to simultaneously hide behind

33

me, and pull me backwards as if to say "We have to get the hell out of here. Let's go!"

I start laughing and cheering and do my best to reassure Wendy that the bull is not going to climb up eight rows of seats to get to us without going through a fence and a lot of other people first. And if he does, Derek and I will kick his ass.

A door is opened in the second circle that lets the bull back into the ring and closes off his advancing charge. The people in the ring swiftly jump back over the side when the bull comes back into the ring. Sadly, when he comes back into the ring, he has broken a horn clean off. He can no longer fight.

When this happens, they give him a few minutes to calm down, and then they release oxen into the ring. He half-heartedly charges a couple of them, but the moment he comes near them they run away. He finds out that no one wants to fight him and starts to calm down. Then the minions open a door out of the ring, the oxen file out, and the bull files out with them, calm as can be.

The next bull to come out is interesting, but nothing special.

Then there is a short intermission and the first matador, about to take on his second and last bull, decides he wants some ears or a tail today.

He comes into the ring and genuflects right in front of us, crosses himself, then **kneels** twenty feet in front of the entrance where the bull will come steamrolling into the ring. He raises the cape in front of his body at arm's length. We are right above where the bulls come out so he is right in front of us.

Wendy grabs my bicep and buries her head in my shoulder. "I can't watch. Lena said the last time a matador did this he got his face ripped off."

I don't know what's coming but it sounds like it must be cool.

Well, he remains there, kneeling in front of the bull gate, his cape spread out in front of him. The gate opens and still he remains kneeling.

Are you kidding me? He's going to kneel in front of the entrance to the next living locomotive?

Yup, he sure is.

The bull comes roaring out at full speed.

Imagine: He has been in a quiet stall with his brothers. He is separated from them and prodded from above a long hallway with a light at the end. Just before he reaches the light, something pricks him between the shoulders. It doesn't hurt, but it is a shock. Quick! Forward! Something must be attacking! In this situation the right answer is always to charge! And so he charges. Into the bright sunlight, momentarily blinded and then he hears a massive roar, the roar of the crowd. He can barely make out something pink and moving through his sun-blinded eyes. Charge it! And he does. The matador gauges the bull, flicks the cape up, quickly to the right, then flings it left, then rolls to the right and, luckily, the bull chooses to follow the pink cape rather than the bright yellow man rolling on the ground.

And the minions emerge from behind walls and are distracting the bull immediately with capes, drawing the bull away from the matador so he can grab his own cape. The bull circles the ring, charging madly at anyone who steps from behind the walls, taunting him as they are instructed to do. He does a complete circle and he is furious. No one will stand and accept his charge! The matador is again alone in the ring with the bull. The bull sees him. The matador again drops to his knees as the bull charges him from fifty yards and he does the pass again, rolling to his side as the bull goes flying over him.

It is unreal.

I cheer until I am hoarse.

And now Derek is hooked too.

The sad part about this is, the bull quickly lost spirit and turned in a very poor performance after this Matador started off the fight so well. So, despite his courage at the start, he could not get a good fight out of the bull and was not awarded ears or a tail. This is important. They keep close track on these things. The more ears and tail you earn in the ring the more your fame grows and the more desired you are as a bullfighter. The more desired bullfighters make tens of thousands of dollars for a one day appearance. The very best in the business can command over a hundred thousand dollars for a day's work.

The next fight is good, but not great.

As usual, the last fight of the night is the most exciting. This is because the oldest most experienced bullfighters fight first, then down in descending order of experience. The youngest men always think they are invulnerable and invincible and take more risks, earning more rewards. And more pain.

The matador comes out ready to fight and gets a dangerous, aggressive bull to match him. He's very good. It is a good fight right up until the part where he gets caught by the bull, thrown into the air, and then when he lands the bull is on him on the ground, mauling him with horns and hooves.

As the saying goes "It's always funny until someone gets hurt. Then it's hilarious."

His minions run in and furiously wave capes in front of the bull, trying to draw him off the matador and eventually they do. The matador stands up, brushes himself off, limps over to his cape, takes a few deep breaths, waves the minions away and starts to fight the bull again.

Now it's an excellent fight.

Wendy tells me that yes, this is normal. They will even take a matador who has been caught by a bull over to the side, sew up his wounds, and he will go back into the ring with stitches and finish his bull. Unless the doctor says the injury is life threatening, he will return to the ring. He will insist.

Outstanding.

He plays with the bull, a bull that has caught him and gored him, for another five minutes before going for the killing sword.

He has blood on his back.

He finishes the bull and the crowd wants him rewarded. The cheers are deafening, and the president assents. He gets an ear and does a slow circle around the ring with his minions. People throw things from the stands to him to touch and his minions throw them back into the crowd.

An amazing day. A day the bulls showed up.

We leave and head to the bull bar up the street we always go to. We stop on the way at the T-shirt and souvenir stands for Derek and me to pick up gifts. As we're leaving, Wendy and Candy walk ahead of us and I look more closely at Derek.

"Dude, you look a little tired."

"After we left your barbeque last night we went to two other bars. I didn't get to sleep until five and then they got me up at ten to go out again. Candy tells me we're going to make tonight an early night."

I laugh in his face. "Derek, I hate to tell you, but you are in Madrid, out with two girls who have completely embraced this lifestyle. There is no such thing as an early night here. Unicorns are seen more frequently than early nights in Madrid. You have miles to go before you sleep my friend. You have miles and miles!"

For I know these women and it is tapas time.

It's almost impossible to be fat living for any length of time in Spain. For one thing, the easiest way to get around is a lot of walking. For another - tapas! Tapas are a huge part of Spanish culture. As near as I can tell, it's the best way to eat since everyone drinks with every meal. And since you go to different bars to get different tapas, you are always walking for more food.

The American equivalent of this would be you and your friends go out to Burger King. You order three beers and they give you a small plate of fries to share. You chat for a bit, eat the fries, walk a couple blocks over to McDonalds and order three more beers and they bring you a cheeseburger sliced into eighths. You chat for a bit, eat some slices of cheeseburger and then take a bus to Pizza Hut. You get three glasses of Rioja and a tiny pizza. And this goes on all night.

Which brings up another cultural difference. You don't usually see that many drunk and rowdy people wandering the streets at night (I saw one, and I don't know if he was drunk or insane) because it is a different style of drinking. No one goes to one bar to stand around and drink all night. Nope. You go to tons of bars with tons of little snacks all night. There will be a lot of conversation, a lot of walking, and a lot of time between drinks.

You can get drunk doing that, but you have to work at it.

We arrive at the bull bar and order some drinks, appetizers, and tapas comes with the drinks.

An older gentleman next to me asks "Excuse me, are you all American?"

We have a fascinating conversation with this man who is both an opera singer, and writer. He has been in Spain for the last month doing research for his next book. We talk attorneys, American men, bullfighting, how beautiful his home country of Wales is, and how many languages he speaks. Which would be five.

I realize Derek has disappeared and find him outside. Derek is talking on his cell phone with the girl who was all over him at the barbeque. He is wondering when we're leaving and he looks exhausted.

I smile. Miles to go buddy. Miles.

Wendy and Candy want to take us to another bull bar that is a bus ride away. We walk up the street to the bus stop and hop on and ride for fifteen minutes to another section of the city. When we get off, there is a shiny bull bar with fake mounted ceramic bull heads in it. It looks like McDonalds with a bar and bullfighting decorations. I want to go in and get some pictures but am told this is a tourist bull bar. The one we're going to is similar but has authentic Spanish people and memorabilia in it.

We get there and I see the difference; now **this** is a bull bar!

Just like the last place, they have gigantic bull heads mounted on the wall, but these are real. They have authentic Spanish wine and beer, atmosphere and a massive variety of tapas! Unlike the other clean and sterile place, they have an entire wall of pictures dedicated to the goring of matadors! They have pictures of bulls on the wrong side of the wall throwing people over the side; pictures of a bullfighter being operated on then dying on the operating table; various pictures of men being lifted into the air on bull horns going through the crotch, the thigh, the shoulder, the stomach. We get some drinks and tapas and I examine an endless line of fascinating photos. I look around after half an hour.

"Hey Derek; how are you doing buddy?" His eyes are almost closed, swaying at the bar.

Welcome to Spain, I think, and chuckle.

Then it's off to Ben and Jerry's for a cone, then a store that sells cigarettes, and then we part company. Wendy and I are heading in one direction towards her apartment and Derek and Candy are supposedly heading to hers. I don't know what time he eventually got to sleep, but I can sympathize.

The next morning, it's time for me to head home.

Suck.

Wendy and I both wake up exhausted for my early flight. She still gets in the cab with me to the airport, stays in line with me while validating tickets and getting asked stupid questions, and then when she can follow and help no more, waves, smiles and blows kisses to me for thirty minutes while I slowly disappear out of sight through the security line. Every time I turn around, she is still there; smiling, radiating love and encouragement.

It was incredibly touching. We were both exhausted, and I know she just wanted to go home and sleep, but instead, she stayed with me for over two hours of waiting, and then, even when she can no longer be by my side, she stays and lets me know she is there for me as I slowly work my way further and further away from her until I finally disappear from sight.

Thus ended my first visit to Madrid.

Christmas in Vermont

In December, Wendy returns to the States for Christmas with her father and to visit me. We spend every second together and split time between my house and her father's house on the lake, reading, watching movies, endlessly talking, and catching up with old local friends, having poker parties (of which Wendy is a natural shark) and talking about the future.

By the time she leaves, I am sure that I will be living in Spain next year. I will follow her anywhere to be with her. In early January she flies back to Madrid.

Longing

Day after day blends into work, then call Wendy and talk for between two and four hours a night. I redouble my efforts at losing weight, compete in a submission wrestling tournament and take second place.

One night, Wendy calls me on the ninety minute drive up to MMA practice.

"What are we waiting for?"

"What do you mean?"

"How come you're not here with me now?"

"My contract with the school runs out in June."

"Yeah, but most contracts allow you to leave with thirty days or even two weeks notice. You could do that and move over here a lot sooner than July."

"That's true. I never thought of that. For some reason I was thinking I needed to work until the contract expired."

"I don't think you do."

"I'll look into it. You sure you're ready to have a roommate?"

Pause.

"Yeah; I am. I really am."

"I'll look into it."

"Have a good practice."

"I love you."

Quiet, almost whispered, longing: "I love you too."

A college friend of mine, Doug, moves into my house with me. Someone will have to watch the house and dogs when I am gone.

Madrid Oddities

A few months ago I subscribed to Vonage, which is an internet phone company that allows me to call Spain over my cable internet connection and talk for as long as I want for one low monthly fee. Good thing too since Wendy and I talk every night. I wonder if we will ever run out of things to talk about. One of the many things we talk about is me quitting the best job I have ever had and moving to Spain.

Despite the fact that I have a house that is fully paid for and a stable job with health insurance, it will be me who has to make the move if we are to be together. Wendy has been in love with Spain since she was fifteen and lived there for a year with her mother. She has been trying to get back there for twenty years and it has finally happened. For the last eighteen months she has had a job in Spain, a beautiful apartment, friends, and the life she has always wanted. An American man with no interest in leaving his living room was the last thing she was looking for at this stage in her life. And yet, here I am. Good thing Spanish men were such a disappointment to her.

I make it through security with zero hassle. Small airports are the best. The guards are having a heated discussion about Taco Bell versus Hooters and have little interest in me. No, I don't understand it either. I sit in the secure area for thirty minutes before we are finally allowed to board. I'm seated next to a good-looking blonde who appears to bc about my age. I smile at her like a spider to a fly.

Twelve years of marriage had taken their toll on my body. I ballooned into a bloated caricature of my former self. Since Marilyn died, I have changed my diet, started running again, bought an exercise bike, a top of the line rowing machine, and started attending mixed martial arts classes. (Which were **brutal** on my forty year old body.) I have also researched proper diet and now eat wheat bread turkey sandwiches and fresh fish instead of Hungry Man frozen dinners and McDonalds.

When you let yourself get forty pounds overweight, and you look in the mirror and give that image the finger because you hate the stranger staring back at you so much, you also stop pretending women might be interested in your company. At least, those of us with a grasp on reality. I'm now thin and getting carded when I buy alcohol in a strange place, thanks to a baby face, so I feel more like my old self when talking to women.

I chat her up, since I've always had an easy manner with the opposite sex.

We sit on the runway for forty-five minutes and I learn we have a lot in common. Her mom died of cancer five years ago. She herself is a cancer survivor. She works in a high school as a computer teacher and is separated from her husband. Right now she is heading to Florida to meet up with a girlfriend she met playing online games. After about thirty minutes of this it's clear she's getting very interested in me and I better clear up some things. I like the chase and winning women over but I don't like to hurt people. So I tell her about Wendy and flying to Madrid. How I'm moving to Madrid in a few weeks. How great she is. Her face droops.

(Am I kidding, or is this artistic license? I don't know, what do you think makes a better story? Just kidding, it's all real. She wants me bad.)

The flight goes fine with no turbulence, and I'm not nervous even though my whiskey wore off long before we even got into the air. I get inside JFK and she's waiting for me.

"Here's my card. I'd love to read your next book when you get it finished."

Yeah baby, thanks but I'm taken.

I grab a quick bite of sustenance, and by the time I get to my terminal, they're already allowing us to board. Some good. And... another delay. We sit on the runway for an hour. Forty-five minutes in the air later they start serving drinks. I'm not very nervous, but I do want to sleep since this is a night flight and I'll be arriving in Madrid in their morning. I get a couple glasses of wine but it still takes me an hour to fall asleep, and I sleep fitfully the whole way there. The whole thing pretty much sucks.

So anyway, I get off the flight, we're thirty minutes late, I get through customs without so much as a glance, and there is my beautiful Spanish girl. She is smiling at me and exclaims "You are so thin Jamie Wakefield!"

Ah, to be back in Madrid. Some good. Preparing to move to Madrid, though, presents more than just logistical problems. What am I going to do without some insanely funny sidekick to entertain my readers? A lot of my success as a Magic writer was the ability to make the reader laugh. I wasn't a good writer; I was a reporter. I've just been blessed to hang out with comedians. It used to be Alan Webster, now it's Joshie. I better hope to find someone funnier than me in Spain who needs a straight man, or my writing is going to suffer. For instance - Thursday is hot and sour soup day with Joshie, Dan, and Sam, the other computer techs for the school system. They are wishing me well on my week away, and subsequent follow-up long term away. Between slurps Joshie says:

"I think you and Wendy are going to make it."
"I think so too; that whole 'madly in love with her' thing kind of helps."
"Unless she has some horrible flaw you're not aware of."
"She doesn't."
"What if she has a penis?"
Laughing - "She doesn't!"
"Well, have you checked?"

How can you respond to that with anything other than a disbelieving stare and then laughter? I could say "Yes, I've been there, there's no penis" but based on the impish grin on his face I'm pretty sure it was a rhetorical question.

We take a taxi back to her beautiful marble floored apartment with the massive terrace looking out over the city. It is about fifty degrees. Coming from the winter weather of Vermont, this is paradise. We spend a great deal of the day sipping wine, talking, and watching movies on a laptop perched on my lap as we lay propped up in bed.

The next few days are very tame. My visit came as a bit of a shock to Wendy. I wanted to surprise her with a visit for her birthday but I'm horrible at keeping secrets and I knew it would be best to tell her so she could prepare. She's too busy on work projects to take an entire week off and I told her that was fine. I wanted to come over and have a "slice of the future" week. To see what life is going to be like while I'm there and we're both working.

I guess it's time to explain Magic. "Magic: The Gathering" is a strategy game invented by Richard Garfield in 1993 that combines elements of chess, poker and fantasy role playing games into an addicting, ever changing card game. The Professional Tour was introduced to help market the game and well over a million dollars in prizes are given away each year with competitions in every corner of the globe. You can't buy your way into the pro tour like the World Series of Poker, you have to earn it. I made myself rather popular on the Internet for my columns about decks, strategies, set reviews and especially tournament reports where I would recount testing, winning, losing, choices I should have made and especially anything hilarious said by any of my friends or opponents. I have been dubbed "The King of the Fatties" for my style of deck-building that incorporates larger creatures than other, better players would consider using. And yet, somehow I have used them to qualify for the Pro Tour three times. I've actually been five times but two of those times didn't require me to win a tournament.

In all honesty, it is my writing, not my playing, that has earned me a small measure of fame in the Magic world.

So this week, I need to do some work as well. I have some writing to do, some testing for the Pro Tour Magic qualifiers, and a column due for Star City Games. We both work during the day then relax in the evening together.

One night Wendy and I are watching "Grey's Anatomy." Burke and Christina are refusing to speak to each other. They still live together. They are still in love. But whoever speaks first is wrong, and feels they are giving up power to the other. I pause the show and look at Wendy.

"We can't have power struggles like that. You need to understand that I'm the man."

"Right, which means you apologize first. I'm glad we're clear on that."

I have found my funny sidekick.

On one middle of the day we decide to go for a walk and grab some Chinese food outside. *Madrileños* are not used to the cold. Everyone around me is wearing winter jackets and I'm sweating in a denim jacket. I am so frikkin hot! It's fifty-five degrees! I take off my socks on the Metro to try and stop sweating. I leave the jacket home the rest of the week and marvel at all the people wearing puffy winter jackets.

Wendy explains to me that the food here will be a little different. Chinese food is adapted for the Spanish culture here, just like it's adapted for the American culture at home. I never really thought about that, but it makes sense. The inside of the restaurant is stunning. There are beautiful paintings on the walls and ceiling with a very nice young couple running the place, and a dozen or so customers. I order some sweet and sour pork, hot and sour soup and shrimp fried rice. (Wendy orders for me and let me tell you, it is odd hearing a Chinese woman speaking Spanish. You just don't expect it. It's also odd hearing Spaniards talk at their dogs telling them to "come" or "sit" or "good boy." I mean, they barely understand commands in English, how do they expect them to learn Spanish?)

The hot and sour soup is okay but not great. Of the six places I have had the soup, it rates about third. It has more veggies and less tofu in it than in any place I've tried in the States. The pork is a little different, but delicious. It is definitely a place we'll return to.

In the evening Wendy and I go out shopping. I'm finally going to make cigala! We head down to the local grocery store because they have a nice fish market and we need a bunch of other things as well. When we get there, I suffer a bit of sticker shock.

58.95 per kilo.

That's in Euros. Considering a Euro is worth 1.33 dollars, that's $78 a kilo.

A kilo is 2.2 pounds.

I'm used to paying $9.95 a pound for lobster. Cigala is $39 a pound.

Ouch.

Wendy suggests we head to another market to check the prices there. We pick up the other things we need at the store and head across town to the other market. It is a collection of little stands all independently owned. They have meat stands, vegetable stands, fish stands, olive stands, and all manner of things. Mostly fish and meat and veggies though. We find a very nice vendor who has cigala for 48.95 a kilo. On the walk over I made my peace with the price of cigala. I remind myself that at home I regularly spent a hundred bucks on lobster dinners for family and friends. I get us a kilo (which amounts to eight of the little buggers), and the man at the stall gives us some bay leaves and tells us to put them in after the cigala have been boiling for a few minutes and we head home.

I'm very excited.

The good news is, the cigala is delicious, but it suffers from the same problem as crab. Not enough meat for too much work. (I'm not talking king crab here, just normal crab.) The tails have a fair amount of meat in them, but after six claws and gaining almost enough meat to fill a tablespoon, we both give up on the claws and just eat the tails. While delicious, there is a large empty hole in the place where our dinner is supposed to be.

I cook up a frozen pizza, Wendy defrosts some shrimp. We watch *The Departed*. It is insane. It is insanely funny, insanely clever, insanely involving and very entertaining. The ending is borderline lame. Nah. That's too kind. The ending was awful.

Tonight's pizza is ham, mushrooms, and black olives.

I take a bite of pizza and get that lovely Spanish crunch and wince. Sometimes when you eat Spanish food, you get a nice crunch in the inside of your mouth, and then a feeling like a tooth has just broken. In Spain, it's quite all right for the chef to mix items that need to be dissected before you eat them into food that should all go into your mouth, chewed, and swallowed.

The black olives aren't pitted.

See, that just baffles me. And it is so typical. They expect you to be eating pizza, stop, set the pizza down, peel the olive, and then go back to eating. It's the same with a bunch of things I've found. Paella is like that. In the middle of a nice soft forkful of rice, you suddenly find a chicken wing, pull it out of your mouth, set your fork aside and eat the chicken off it, and put the bone on the side. The mussels still have the shell with them. The cigala isn't cigala meat, it's the whole thing, shell and all, mixed right into the rice.

I find this baffling. Wendy finds it charming.

Life is good. Each day is work, break, work, sip wine, watch TV or read, talk until the wee hours of the night, awake late morning.

One day we decide to go out for a run. This is something both of us are curious as to how it will work. I like to meditate while running. Wendy likes to listen to her iPod. I don't run as far as she does, but I run faster. We're both used to running alone and I haven't had a running partner since college. But, as with everything else, it all works out just fine. I slow my pace a little bit and discover I can go much farther and more endorphins get released. I'm told you also lose more weight this way. It is easier on the knees and better for your body. I find it is also better for your mind as I am not struggling so hard and can meditate easier.

The architecture of Spain continues to amaze me. We start out running by the hundred yard long Royal Palace with its dozens of statues along the roof, perched in front, and across the park across the street. Down below, I spy yet another garden and park. We run farther on and past another park with a fifty foot tall statue of Don Quixote and Sancho Panza then up a seemingly endless hill, and across to another park with an Egyptian temple in it. The temple park is a large circle, perfect for running. Even though it is nearly dark, there are kids playing, families and old couples strolling along, people walking their dogs, and other runners.

All the while Wendy is explaining the significance and history of everything around us. Why the Temple de Diebold is here, what's inside the palace, how old it is, why there is so much French architecture across from the castle and who Don Quixote is. No wait, I knew that last one… BFA in Writing for the win!

We circle the park three times and then jog back down the hill, back past Don Quixote, back past the palace and the parks and finally home. Now it is time for some water, a shower and then some relaxation in front of the TV, or maybe a walk and then a chat at a little café and some people-watching. Ah, life is good in Madrid.

I knew things would be different in Madrid, but some things are a lot more different than I expected.

Did you know that there is no Sprint or Verizon Wireless here? I thought those were global companies. Nope. I need a whole new provider when I move over here. Good thing I just signed a new two year cell phone contract in the states only six months ago.

You know what families do on a Sunday night? They all go out for a stroll. Can you imagine being in an American city and eleven o'clock at night there are entire families going for a leisurely walk?

Milk isn't refrigerated until opened. Wendy has three gallons in her cupboard.

Eggs are not refrigerated.

When I pour cream into my coffee, the expiration date is five months away.

Spaniards love T-shirts with English written on them. Despite the fact that eighty percent of *Madrileños* actually speak little to no English, seeing a T-shirt with Spanish on it is rare. English T-shirts are everywhere. What's hilarious is the bungled English on the shirts. Sometimes they say something simple like "Kiss Me" or "Your boyfriend wants me." But usually they say something nonsensical like "Pet my bany" with a picture of a "bunny" on it. What does that even mean? Are you carrying a "bany" with you somewhere? Is there a part of the body you think English speakers refer to as their bunny? Or the one Wendy saw yesterday "My Planet – Right or Wrong." What? Like you have a choice? You support your planet whether it's right or wrong? What? "My Planet – Love it or leave it?" Our friend Dawn wants to make a T-shirt that says "You don't have the faintest idea what this says, do you?"

When you go into a market and there is no line, just people standing around waiting you say *"Quien es la ultima'"* (Who is last?) Then, when the next person asks, you tell them that you are. This is the closest thing to a line you will ever find in Spain.

Madrid is so dry you don't even need a clothes dryer. You can hang up a shirt and have it be dry by the end of the day. Clotheslines flourish in Madrid.

Lights are on timers, like most of Europe. America has been spoiled by their low cost energy. When Wendy and I come home and the stairway is dark, we turn on a light and it goes off automatically about thirty seconds after we get inside our apartment. When you go into a restaurant or bar's bathroom the light is on a timer. You bang the timer with your hand then hit the stall and halfway through your business the light goes off and you're peeing in the dark. Most of the time it's a simple matter to reach over and bang the timer again, but not always. The timers have little nightlights on them so you know where to push but sometimes those lights have burned out. Sometimes the switch is actually outside the door, or outside the stall you're in. This makes things much more difficult. I have literally been trapped in a bathroom before, unable to find the door or the light switch to illuminate the way out. After seven minutes of stumbling around, feeling the walls with my hands I desperately thought "Doesn't anyone else in this God-forsaken restaurant have to pee and can open the door so I can get out of here?"

Spaniards love their noise like no one else on the planet. Nowhere is this more evident than in a toilet stall. For some reason, the toilet paper holders have noisemakers on them. They all have flaps of loud, loosely fitted metal over the roll and every time you take more paper, it bangs, loudly. If you rip off a good amount, tugging three or four times for paper everyone can hear this "CLANG CLANG CLANG!" coming from your stall as if a signal to all within earshot -

"I'm wiping!"

"I'm wiping again!"

"Yup, one more time! CLANG CLANG CLANG!"

Tipping percentage is very small or nothing. On a fifty Euro check you might leave two or three Euros as a tip.

Spaniards refuse to drink beer that is not freezing ice cold. The taps in the bars are covered with condensation and sometimes the bottoms of the taps have frost collected on them.

Spaniards will mix anything with alcohol. A "shandy" is a mix of lemon soda with beer. A *"tinto verano"* is red wine mixed with Sprite or Seven-up. I don't even know what the name of the drink is when they mix Pepsi and red wine. I think it's called "disgusting."

Living statues are everywhere. I walked by a mono colored statue. It appeared covered in mud or wet clay. Wendy says, "Ah, a living statue."

"Wait. What? That's a person?"

"Yes."

I look closer. There's a small plate of coins in front of her. I drop three coins into the plate. Her hand raises slowly, robot like and waves to me once. It takes thirty seconds. I can't stop giggling.

Being from a small town and only occasionally visiting the city, beggars are something new to me and here, they come in a wide variety.

A guy with a dog, a cell phone, a blanket and a sign that said "Yes I smoke, yes I have a cell phone, but my little dog needs an operation. Please give."

A guy with a sign saying "Yes, I am going to spend it on whiskey - at least I'm honest."

An old woman hunched over and kneeling as if life has beaten her down. She is weathered and rain-battered with a small bowl in front of her for coins; almost completely covered by shawl and blanket, her head on the ground, arms out in front of her constantly wailing and pleading.

A man with no arms, shaking his cup in his teeth and screaming over and over how he needs money. Wendy says he's in the same spot every day.

My favorite is an ethereal attractive young girl kneeling on her shoes in the rain. She isn't even in the square, just a side-street with little traffic. Hand out-stretched, no bowl like most beggars, just her hand. She locks eyes with me as we come out of the grocery store fifty feet away and watches me until I can't take it anymore. I walk over, hand her a couple Euros and she smiles beatifically at me. She watches us walk away until we're out of sight.

Wendy has a slight bent towards geeky things, and I am gently fanning that flame. In our earlier courtship, she went onto the web and read everything there was to read from me and about me. So, naturally, we talked about Magic a bit. She was stepping off the Metro one day a few weeks ago and some kids had binders out and were trading.

"I asked them if they were Magic cards and they were! I had never seen them here in Spain!"

"Cool. Did you tell them you were dating the King of the Fatties?"

"What? No. Why would people in Spain know you? You write for an American site, right?"

"Yeah, but it's on the Internet. You know; international and all that. They might have known me."

"Get over your bad self."

I'll show her.

It is Wendy's birthday today. I have asked the readers of my "Magic: The Gathering" column to please wish her a "Happy Birthday!" on her blog. They did not disappoint; in fact, they amazed. She received an even one hundred well wishes, from all over the world: Malaysia, Japan, Germany, Norway, Brazil, The Netherlands, Australia, Costa Rica, Spain, France, Mexico, Italy, Serbia, Sweden and of course a bunch from the good old US of A.

It was staggering and a great way to start the morning.

We have an appointment at two p.m. at Medina Mayrit. Medina Mayrit is an ancient Arabic bath from the time when the Moors controlled Spain.

Spain has had a long and storied history, constantly being conquered, reclaimed, conquered and claimed again, carving its way into the nation it is today.

It started out under Roman dominion, then in the middle ages came under Germanic control and still later was conquered by Muslims. Spanish Christians in the North were lackadaisical about taking Spain back. They slowly made their way south over a period of over six-hundred years, slowly reclaiming Spain from the Moors. Spaniards reclaimed the last Moorish city "Granada" in 1492; a very good year for Spaniards.

One of my favorite quotes as the last Moorish King looked back at the kingdom he had lost comes from his comforting mother: "Weep like a woman for that which you could not hold onto as a man."

Thanks Mom!

For just under seventy Euros, two people get ninety minutes worth of bathing in three different temperature pools, a dry sauna, and a thirty minute massage.

Wendy and I get our instructions and then go to the changing rooms. We meet in the hallway outside, and make our way downstairs to the pools. There is a large tub that reminds me of a Vermont mountain spring pool because the water is just above freezing. There is a lukewarm, almost body temperature pool, and a hotter pool that takes a few seconds to ease into. There is also tea and water from spigots and a steam room for baking yourself like a Christmas turkey. All the doorways and ceilings are arched and light filters in from small holes in the ceiling. The scent of jasmine fills the air.

We start with the lukewarm pool, and it is wonderful. We float a bit and hug and swim around slowly in the four foot water. Then we move to the hot pool, and for some reason we can't stop smiling. We are bathing in so much history, and the sight of the place is so Arabic in design and so quiet and reverent and relaxing. The hot pool is like a hot tub twenty feet across and fifty feet in length. Relaxation flows through us. Once we're almost passed out from that, Wendy motions for the cold pool. I assent and we head across the hall to a large tub, maybe three feet across, three feet deep and eight feet long.

We slowly climb into it, trying to acclimate. Oh my God it is so cold! Wendy does her best to sink under the surface of the water but can't force herself. I decide I will show her how manly I am and just dunk my head under like it is nothing. Fat chance. I sink down to my chest and involuntarily grunt and almost scream.

"Whoohrrrerahhhh" I say through gritted teeth.

"What was that?" Wendy asks.

"Nothing dear, nothing at all; shall we try the steam room?"

"Good idea."

The steam room is amazing. Unlike a sauna, this is a wet heat and doesn't burn your lungs as you breathe; hence, it is much more comfortable. The heat is to the point of over-powering when you first get in there, then you just lay back and enjoy the warmth spreading through your body and deep down into your bones. I sit there and bake, sweat pouring off me as if I am being basted. I let the last six months of my life wash over me: this wonderful woman, this beautiful city, the gigantic, intricate artwork and statues, bullfighting, flying. Lying in bed and sipping wine and watching movies and talking until two-thirty in the morning. I lean over and whisper in Wendy's ear –

"Thank you for taking me on all these amazing adventures."

"I wouldn't do this alone. Thank you for being with me."

We eventually return to the lukewarm pool, and then a woman peaks her head in and asks what the numbers are on our bracelets. We're who she is looking for so it's time for our massage. We are led upstairs and there are three masseuses, two men and a woman. Wendy gets a guy, I get a guy, and the woman with us gets the woman.

"Uh, Wendy, can you ask them if it's not too much trouble to switch us? I really prefer to get rubbed down by a woman."

Honestly, who can ever forget the "George getting a massage from a man" scene in *Seinfeld*?

It's no problem and I get the girl. (Of course, I always get the girl.) We have a half hour massage that is bliss. Then we have fifteen minutes left downstairs and we're done. We walk home, completely relaxed and smiling. Wendy tells me "We should bring your folks there."

"Yes, we should. They'll love it."

We head home and relax for a bit, and then it's time for mojitos and dinner with Wendy's friends. Birthday dinner for Wendy! She turns thirty-nine this year.

We show up at the bar specializing in mojitos and Dawn is already there, taking notes and working on her plan for this year. She runs a bike touring company and this year is going to branch out into self-publishing guides for week and weekend trips. She's very excited. We're going to set her up with Joshie when he comes to visit. We're soon joined by Kinga, Lena and Stefan, Candy, and Alana who are all ex-pats and all English speaking.

Lena and Stefan show up smiling and each wearing a shirt with Wendy's picture on it that says "40-1".

Mojitos are had by all, and then we move down two doors to the restaurant where we'll be having dinner. A variety of wine is ordered. A variety of food is ordered. Dinner is pretty much insane. There are eight people at the table and five loud, passionate conversations going on at once. The food is delicious and varied. We order two or three plates of food that all have a selection of choices on them. We have grilled vegetables and pineapple, mushrooms, sausage, quail, bits of steak, chicken and fish with guacamole. Then we follow Wendy's family tradition of ordering every dessert on the menu and everyone has a bite and passes it to the left until everyone is sick, or the desserts are gone.

After dinner, a few people take off, and a few of us head to a disco, but it's closed, so we settle for the bar next to it. Alana is President of "Democrats Abroad" and we have a passionate discussion on the last six years of American politics and who should be president in 2008, Obama or Clinton. I would say debate except for the fact that we agree with each other on everything.

Then it's back home and some sleep.

Friday was work and recover from Wendy's birthday dinner.

Wendy is lying in bed reading. I have just stepped out of the shower, combed my hair and I'm drying myself off. In the process of doing so, I find a rogue chest hair, located on the top left hand corner of my chest, almost to the shoulder, it is silver, and six inches long. I'll have to have Wendy pluck that for me. I come out of the bathroom and ask Wendy -

"Hey, want to see something gross?"

She doesn't even look up from her book "Not if you ever want to have sex with me again."

I laugh out loud and decide I can pluck this myself. Beautiful and witty; I have definitely found my new sidekick.

Saturday was return home.

Suck.

As I get on the plane for home, I see that once again, I am seated next to an attractive young woman. This time she is a little bit younger than I am. I'm always glad to be sitting next to women because I communicate much better with women than men. She is reading and doesn't even look up as I sit down. I pull out a Time, Wired, and my current book on bullfighting, "Death and the Sun."

We sit there not talking for an hour until I see the author of her book. "Oh. Chris Bohjalian."

"Excuse me?"

"I was just noticing the author of your book; Chris Bohjalian. He lives ten miles up the road from me."

She grunts and goes back to her book. I check my pits. Hmm, I smell fine.

The snack tray comes around and she puts her book down and gets some cookies.

"So, what were you doing in Spain?"

"Just traveling."

She quickly picks up her book.

"I was visiting my girlfriend."

She puts her book down.

"Oh yeah? Then this must be rough for you?"

"A little but I'll be back in three weeks to move in with her."

No longer threatened, she opens up to me. I draw her out for about ten minutes, asking questions about her. Everyone's favorite subject is themselves. Finally I say:

"Want to hear my Chris Bohjalian story?

"Sure!"

It happened about ten years ago. He lives up the road about ten minutes away and back in the day when everyone was on dial-up, the phone lines near him were primitive and awful so he couldn't hold a connection. It dropped the line all the time. Since he was a good customer of the computer store I was working at, they sent me up to hook up an external modem that holds a connection better. So, I walk in, and his house is nothing special. Nothing bad either, just modest. Except for his study which has hardwood floors, bookcases on all four walls with all the books in hardcover. An eight-foot wooden table sits in the center of the room with a computer, scanner, and printer attached. On the floor, to the right of the huge desk, is a stack of *New York Times* and *People* magazines. These are the ones that reviewed his book (NYT), and talked about how great he was on Oprah (People).

I start to get to work and he asks if I want a Coke. I say sure, thanks, and he goes to get it. The phone rings while he's in the other room, and he is chatting on it when he comes back into the room. He sets my Coke on the floor and wanders around talking, eventually going back into the kitchen. I get the modem all attached in the back and move to the front of the table. On the way there, I forget about the Coke on the floor and kick it over.

Splashing Coke all over his stacks of *New York Times* and *People* magazines.

Skah!
I rush into the kitchen and interrupt him.
"I need paper towels. Fast!"
He casually hands them to me and continues talking. He has to know what's going on. I rush back into the room and clean up my mess. And, having done all of that, I have to finish setting up the modem and face his wrath when he gets off the phone.

He never says a word in anger or acknowledgement of my accident that he could clearly see from his kitchen. He gets done his conversation, I test the modem, it holds a signal for a few minutes, he thanks me and I head back to work.

"Nice guy, huh?"
"Yeah! Sounds like it," she replies.
"Yup, he was always great. I found out later that he's very anal, so, spilling Coke all over his stuff must have made him crazy. He would come into the store, open up his laptop, and then wipe his fingerprints off it. Move the mouse, wipe the fingerprints off.

"Wow."

"Yeah."

Now she likes talking to me and her book is forgotten. She's married with two kids and truly, madly, deeply in love with her husband. She's done over a hundred dives, and is an advanced scuba diver like Wendy. She went skydiving once and wasn't that thrilled with it. For the suiting up, the ride in the plane, it's not a long enough thrill. As I mentioned, everyone's favorite subject is themselves. As long as you offer the slightest encouragement, they will happily tell you their life story. I have used this observation over the years to get women to like me, even though I've never said a word about *me*, just let them talk. (Just a little tip for you single guys out there, just continually ask questions until she asks one back, then steer the conversation back to them after a brief answer. You can tell them all about how great you are later.) She loves white water rafting. She is a physical therapist who works with kids. She loves her job. Her dog died a year ago and she still misses him

We talk for about sixty minutes and then I start thinking "Okay, it was fun winning you over, but I need a nap soon."

At a break in the conversation I lay my head back and close my eyes. About thirty minutes later she gets the hint and I sleep for an hour. She wakes me up and she tells me the movie sucks and I have to entertain her.

Why am I cursed with being so good with women?

Cursed.... Yeah.... .

Now I am home and back at work. We're interviewing people for my position in the district. My best friend and co-worker Josh is in fine form the day of the interviews. We're singing *Futurama's* Bender's theme song of "I love lootin', I love stealin'," and quoting web comics as we walk into the main office.

"The Iractonians have been defeated! The planet itself rumbles in triumph!"

"Hey lover, want to learn how to hide a body?"

"Boy, do I!"

We're not very thrilled with the resumes, but we have some that show promise. We call six people in for interviews. Dan, Sam, me, Joshie, and our boss Patricia are all meeting them. Josh keeps bitching at me for leaving to start a new life. Sam keeps saying, "I can't believe you're leaving." Dan says, "I hope these interviews show us someone with potential."

"Yeah, let's hope we don't get any more like Frank Dred," Josh replies.

"Who? I don't remember him."

"You know, he's the guy who spelled his name three different ways on his resume, came in wearing bloody gloves and his eyes glazed over and he licked his lips when we mentioned he might have to work with kids."

This is met with riotous laughter from all of us. The scary thing is, while that was actually an exaggeration, we all know the man he is referring to.

Patricia goes upstairs and gets our first candidate. He comes down, well dressed, but not overdressed. Good mannerisms. Not geeky at all. He aces the interview. We are all literally blown away by his answers, obvious skill and hoping he doesn't find another job before we offer him this one.

He leaves.

Dan looks at me and smiles, "What are you still doing here, Wakefield?"

He's that good.

"Jesus, Josh, I thought you were going to polish that guy's knob by the time the interview was done," Sam says.

"Hey, that guy is perfect. We can assign him all the tasks and take a month off. He can do it all," Josh replies.

Josh feels great relief now that he has someone cool and knowledgeable to work with. He's been dreading what we might find to replace me. We all agree the other interviews will be worthless, but we have to go through the process.

The next guy comes down in a suit. Good thing because we're very professional. Josh is wearing an Adidas sweatshirt and I'm in a black UFC T-shirt. He's really not good for the job and we know it by the time Patricia escorts him out.

"If I have to work with that guy, one morning there's going to be a large, heavy black plastic bag in the school dumpster."

"Did you notice he didn't actually answer any of the questions, no matter how much he talked?"

"Did you notice that he gave a ten minute answer to every question except for 'Do you have any problem working with kids?' -

and on that one he paused for fifteen seconds and then said 'I have no problem with that.'"

The jokes just keep flying. Josh reduces us to tears and Patricia does her best to rein us in, but she can't stop laughing herself. Her face is beet-red she's laughing so hard. After about her third attempt, Josh takes over. "Okay, we're going to have to be serious about this. We're all going to calm down and act like professionals."

Dan is incredulous: "Josh, why are you looking at me?" The absurdity of Josh telling us that causes us all to start laughing again. Patricia finally gets herself under control.

"Alright, I'm going to go up and get the next candidate. Think calming thoughts. Jamie, you think about Madrid; Josh, you think about Pokemon or whatever damn thing will calm you down."

The next candidate is also awful. He leaves and Josh says, "Look, I took your advice and kept myself sane by drawing Pokemon guys."

He lifts up his notes and shows us his drawings.

There is more riotous tearful laughter.

In total, we got one person who is perfect; one who can do the job and be acceptable; one that can't do the job but could be trained and has a great attitude. The others are just three complete duds.

The Narnia Chapter

February 16th was my last day of gainful employment.

What a scary thing to type.

The plan was to take a week off and relax before I start the next chapter of my life. Life is always about chapters. The high school chapter. The college chapter. The eight years at the Middlebury Inn chapter. The married chapter. The computer tech chapter. The cancer chapter. Ugh. That chapter sucked with a capital Suck.

The plan for the week off was to play some Magic, zone out in front of the TV and play poker with my friends. It was going to be great. Instead I spent the next week running around like a madman taking care of things that I had no idea I would need to manage before I left. But now I am off for a relaxing week in Captiva, Florida with my new love. My parents have become what are known as "snowbirds." Each year they fly down to their favorite little hut in this little marina and relax, escape the Vermont winters and enjoy the ocean. When the stock market is good they'll spend two months down there before coming back to Vermont, and hopefully, the beginnings of spring.

Captiva is amazing. Wendy and I have this little cabin in Jensen's Marina that has manatees floating around the docks. There are dozens of manatees, sometimes within arm's reach. Pelicans wander around the docks, some of them as tall as my thigh. A dozen or more of them gather each afternoon for naptime at the end of the dock. This morning, I look out my window to see a dolphin jump out of the water.

As usual, I can't stop making comparisons and observations. The differences between Madrid and Southern Florida are starker than those of Vermont and Madrid. Madrid is a dry heat. Bath towels and hair dry in minutes. South Florida is remarkably humid. Bath towels never dry. Sunglasses steam up. Clothes that have never been worn feel damp. While everything in Madrid is open late into the night, the general store on this little island closes at six. They roll the streets up at nine. Wendy and I have a rough time staying awake past ten since everyone and everything, including us, gets up at seven in the morning. Where Madrid has cobblestones, mythical statues and the occasional dog, Florida is beach, manatees, dolphins, alligators and a billion species of birds.

And then there is the work ethic. In Captiva, I constantly feel like I am annoying anyone who serves me in any way. The pace of work from waiting tables to checking out at the grocery store is glacial and sullen. It takes us twenty minutes to get an ice cream cone with all of four people ahead of us. I just about go insane.

That said, Florida is the relaxation I was looking for the previous week. I play almost no Magic and watch no TV. No working out. No running. No writing. No phone calls. Instead it is long walks through nature preserves with my parents narrating and my brother John and his son Sammy fishing whenever they find water. Our afternoons and sunsets are usually on the beach. There are margaritas and mojitos, fishing on the dock or even on a boat day trip and chatting with the family. We lie in bed in our little hut and watch movies on Wendy's laptop. We have lunch and dinner at different restaurants around the island with the family. We do some reading and go see "Volver" with my parents and I fall in love with Penelope Cruz. It is all very calm and soothing.

One day we go on a walk through the J. N. "Ding" Darling National Wildlife refuge specifically so my folks can show us some alligators.

"So, where are these alligators?" I ask.

Dad replies "Just off the path up here."

"You know alligators eat people right?"

Mom and Dad shrug.

"The biggest alligator we saw in here was lying across the path. We turned the corner and there it was. John turned and began to run the other way and I grabbed his arm: "Wait, let's get a picture first.""

"That's awesome. Where are we going next, the tiger park?"

We meet a nice couple along the path.

"Afternoon, how are you?" my dad asks.

"Good, good. And you?"

"Very good. Any alligators up ahead?"

"Yes, there are two of them off to the side on the left."

Wendy whispers in my ear, "Of course they're good. There were six in their group when they started walking."

We end up having a very nice relaxing walk through alligator-infested lands and no one dies! We also see some nice big birds and a turtle orgy.

I want to see how dangerous alligators really are so I head for the internet when we return to our cabin. How many people do they kill a year? Well, in 2006 they only killed three people. So, not that many, but still some. Here's something interesting I found though:

"Robert Steele - attacked by an alligator while walking his dog on a trail between two wetland areas in the J.N. "Ding" Darling National Wildlife Refuge near Sanibel, Florida. Steele bled to death after his leg was bitten off below the knee."

Dear Mom and Dad,
Be careful!
Love,
Jamie

On Saturday, John and his family leave for home, and Wendy and I rent a car to drive across the state and visit her friend Laura from law school and her husband. They were an absolute delight and we went out to the world famous "Joe's Stone Crab" for dinner. The wait to get in is two hours long, so we sit by a small fountain in the waiting area, have drinks, appetizers and fine conversation. Wendy is astonished when I explain that the crabs are caught, a claw is torn off then the crab is thrown back into the sea to regenerate. It takes eighteen months to regenerate the limb. Presumably, it is then caught again and the process repeated.

When we do get to eat, the crab is one of the sweetest, most succulent things I have ever had the pleasure to devour.

The next day, we drive to the Miami airport and get there two hours ahead of time. We immediately jump into a line that is a hundred yards long just to get boarding passes and drop off luggage. Then there is a three hundred yard line to get through security. We have to be pulled out of the line and rushed through security by an American Airlines representative to make our flight. But we make it.

Eight hours later and I have officially moved to Madrid.

Let the adventure begin.

The Year of Living Dangerously

Happy New Year to me! It is March 5th, 2007, I have moved to Madrid to start a year of living dangerously. Not "mixed martial arts" dangerous and not "bullfighting" dangerous, but unknown dangerous. I'm talking real terror scary.

Trying to make your living as a writer is scary. It is a journey littered with failure. Everyone wants to be a writer. Everyone thinks they can be a writer. 99.9% of them fail. A recent article in *Time* magazine stated "There are more people who want to be writers than there are people who want to be readers." Do you know that very small literary agencies can get up to five thousand requests a year for representation, and will add less than five of those to their list of clients? So far, I have contacted fifteen agents and have fifteen rejection letters to show for it.

Go me.

But I am not without resources. I brought five books to Spain with me.

"Be Your Own Literary Agent."

"The Everything Get Published Book."

"The Freelance Writer's Bible"

"Odd Thomas" (a gift from a close friend and former girlfriend.)

"Sex and the Perfect Lover" (my backup plan.)

It's now "one year" time. New Year's Day. I have a year to either make it as a writer or else I'll have to turn to selling myself to fat Spanish women. It's just a little bit scary. Actually it's terrifying. Have you seen fat Spanish women?

My first morning living in Madrid, the sun streams in the open window. It is nine-thirty. The alarm went off at eight, Wendy banged it, went back to sleep. Ah, the joys of being a couple who works from home. I'm awake because Wendy just got out of bed, went somewhere, and has now returned and is standing over me staring. I look up at her sleepily and smile. She sighs and gets back into bed.

"You are an evil tempter."

"What? What did I do? I'm just laying here naked and warm."

"That's why you're an evil tempter."

"Without actually doing anything, I'm an evil tempter?"

"Yes."

"What if I was to grab you and pull you into bed and beg you to sleep longer and ignore the clock?"

"Then you would be a horrible evil tempter."

"Ah, I see. If I make an effort, I get upgraded to horrible."

"Yes."

"You know what I just noticed?"

"What?"

"You have green eyes."

"Yes I do. So?"

"In Magic, I am known as the master of all things green."

"So?"

"The eyes are the windows to the soul."

"So, you're my master?"

"That's what I'm thinking."

"Do with me as you will."

My thought when I arrived here was to keep to a rigidly defined schedule. I would get up, have some coffee, then go out to the terrace and do some Pal Dan Gum (ancient meditative stretching) while looking out over the city. After that there would be push-ups, then maybe some weeping from the pain. After that, more coffee, and then I'd work on Spanish by doing lessons in "The Rosetta Stone" for Spain. After that, the most perfect complex carbohydrates in the world, a bowl of oatmeal, then, to "The Writing!"

Oh, the best laid plans of mice and men. Nothing works out the way it should. Life is just too busy. There are too many plans, too many things to get done: health insurance to get, scouring the city for a new monitor, keyboard and USB hub for Wendy's laptop, laundry, shopping, dishes, and endless things that arise unexpectedly.

"Are you always this neat?" Wendy asks. "I mean, you're constantly picking up, doing dishes, doing laundry. Is this just how you are, or is this the product of thirteen years of marriage?"

"Fact. In order, the top three things that couples fight about are sex, money, and housework. We're great at the first two; I'm not interested in fighting about the third."

Then we plan and host a "Welcome to Madrid" party with seventeen of Wendy's closest friends, watch some *Grey's Anatomy* and examine "The Corte Ingles" for food I like, which is a twenty minute walk away. And soon, the bull fights. The days are just packed.

We're getting there though. We are finally getting done all the chores that need to be taken care of when someone moves in with you or in my case, moves to another country and needs certain things he didn't realize he would need. With no car, I am tote-and-carry boy. For the past week, we have done so much shopping that I am constantly walking the streets of Madrid with twenty pounds in each hand. My shoulders are actually sore from carrying things.

"You brought me here just to carry things and satisfy your lustful urges, didn't you?"

"It's true. You have found me out."

"I'm okay with that."

And thus the Four Commandments are born.

1) Keep Wendy warm.
2) Carry heavy things.
3) Satisfy Wendy's lustful urges.
4) Keep Wendy's wine glass filled.

These are the commandments I have made for myself.

Philosophy

We are finally getting settled in and into a routine where we can actually get some work done. Pal Dan Gum has been done a couple times. I'm on section one, chapter seven in Rosetta Stone. I actually spent yesterday playing Magic and wrote a column about it. Wendy went back to work for her company.

We're getting there.

Will I be able to actually move forward on a writing career? Could it be? Will I finally be able to do that? Sometimes I find it maddening. Sure, all the stuff I mentioned needs to be done, but I should be working on being a writer. As my housemate Doug quotes from his ancient scripture in his quest for enlightenment "Jamie there is no should."

I'm still working on being in the moment.

I find that the only way to get better at this is to practice. To realize when your attention is drifting and forcibly pull yourself back. As with almost everything else in the world, it is a matter of will. I've been looking on the web for a snazzy explanation of what that means, and nothing fits, so I'll just do my best to explain what I know. "Being in the moment" means not thinking about the past or the future. It means being present in what you are doing at this moment. Since birth, people are trained to be in the future or in the past, and rarely in the present.

"Big test Friday, better study."

"Bills are due. Been avoiding them for days, better pay them."

"Wow. I was so embarrassed. That haunts me to this day."

All of those are examples of not "being in the moment."

Being in the moment is great for mental health. The past is nothing. The mistakes you made long ago only haunt you if you let them. Every day the slate is cleaned anew and you can build your life from that moment forward. Embarrassments are not to be dwelled on. They are over. They hurt you only because you let them. What matters is learning from them, moving on, and living today.

Clear your mind for a second and trust me. Close your eyes and take a deep breath before moving on to the next paragraph. Ask yourself "Is this a good moment?" This one right now as you read this. Are you warm? Threatened? Hungry? Have you had enough coffee?

It's true. Yes, you have bills to pay. Yes, you have work to do. Yes, relatives are coming to visit this weekend. Yes, you moved to Madrid and have done nothing but chores and settled in and even spent too much time relaxing in bed with your wonderful girlfriend. And now you're beating yourself up over it.

But is this a good moment? This one right this second? Don't worry about the future. Don't dwell on the mistakes of the past. Right now, this second, in the present, pretending the future and the past do not exist, is this a good moment?

Take a breath. Think about the clothes on your body. Think about the seat under your ass. Think about your breath flowing into you. Think about this second. Is it a good second?

That's being in the moment.

"With the past, I have nothing to do; nor with the future. I live now." -Ralph Waldo Emerson.

In practice, I try to remember to think about each moment, to think about right now. I could dwell on the cancer my wife fought last year and the horror of that experience. Or think about the fact that my money is going to run out in the future if I don't get busy and make it as a writer. I could think about the fact that I am sucking at Magic right now and I see no end in sight.

Or I could think about this moment right now.

I'm not in any pain. I'm in a city I love. It's dark both inside and out. Only monitors illuminate the space around me. Next to me, Wendy is lying on the couch browsing the internet on her laptop. I'm warm. I'm sipping a fine red wine from the Rioja region, and I'm doing what I love, which is writing. My pants fit, my shirt is very cool, and I'm having no trouble breathing. My legs are sore from running and that's good. I'm hungry, and that's good too because we're going out to dinner soon.

This moment is good.

The more you focus on the present, the less time your mind has to dwell on the past, or worry about the future. The more you dwell on the present, the more concentrated you are on what is happening in the now.

"Do not dwell in the past; do not dream of the future, concentrate the mind on the present moment." -Buddha

And I know I need to do this because I know what I am.

(The following scenes are recreated as best as I could reconstruct them. They are not exact.)

Preston Burke, the world famous heart surgeon (on Grey's Anatomy) is about to operate for the second time on his musical hero, Eugene Foote, world famous violist.

Preston – "Why do you want me to operate? Your heart is fine."

Eugene – "There is a murmur. A tremor. It throws my playing off."

Preston – "Your playing is fine."

Eugene – "Hand me my violin."

Preston does so and Eugene plays a beautiful piece.

Eugene – "What did you think?"

Preston – "It was beautiful."

Eugene – "Here's what you really thought. You thought 'that man has no right to call himself Eugene Foot.' That's what you thought, and that's what I think."

Preston – "You could die. You are still a master. Let this go."

Eugene – "I am no longer myself. I would rather die on the operating table than no longer be Eugene Foot. Fix me, Preston."

Preston sets his arm on his shoulder.

Preston – "I'll do my best."

"Everything - a horse, a vine - is created for some duty... For what task, then, were you yourself created? A man's true delight is to do the things he was made for." -Marcus Aurelius.

I find Poker boring. Not the games around my dining room table with the buddies, with the drinking and the trash talking and the punching and the kicking and the vomiting. No, those are good times. But playing poker to make money? Playing Poker online and knowing the odds and the math behind pot odds bore me. Folding hands endlessly waiting for the one nut draw is not my thing.

My former roommate and current house caretaker Doug Shepardson plays poker six to twelve hours a day. He has read eleven books on improving his poker. He has a notebook full of notes on his real life opponents, analyzing mistakes he has made, recording his win percentages and reasons why he might have lost to analyze later. He will join a three-thousand-person tournament at ten in the evening and regularly not finish until two or even four in the morning.

He makes a good housemate. We used to get up in the morning, have some coffee, do some Pal Dan Gum, and watch some DVR TV from the previous night. After that, the card flopping would start. His cards with two colors on them, mine with millions. His tournaments with hundreds if not thousands of players, mine with dozens. No TV, no music, no distractions. Each determined to forge our destiny in card flopping.

"Here is a test to find out whether your mission in life is complete. If you're alive, it isn't." -Richard Bach

I used to train in mixed martial arts at a place called Rail City MMA. My instructor was a man named Tom Murphy. He is a six foot two, two hundred and twenty seven pound Atlas of a man. You may think that six foot two doesn't qualify for the status of Atlas, but then, you have never been hit by this man. Admittedly, I have never been truly "hit" by Tom, but more, lightly tapped and kicked to demonstrate a move; lightly, but with enough force to demonstrate that you want to put your weight behind it; lightly but with enough pressure so that I could feel the man's raw power. The tightly wound cords he calls muscles attached to the thick steel rods he refers to as bones.

At the end of class one day, I asked about his history. His eyes flashed when he talked of fighting. When he talked of past wrestling and jiu jitsu matches he had. (He's never lost a match in a jiu jitsu tournament.) He finished up my little post practice interview telling me about how obsessed he was with fighting. How walking down the street he would be thinking of moves, doing katas in his mind as he walked and then becoming aware that people were staring at him and realizing he was doing them on the sidewalk. He told of how he sometimes had trouble focusing on movies because his mind would drift to combat. At work he would plan which of his instructional combat DVDs he would watch when he got home. He had trouble falling asleep. Lying in bed, picturing an imaginary opponent and what he would do if his opponent attacked this way, or did a leg sweep or how he would take him down, pass guard and get him into a kimora. Or rain down elbows if they were allowed.

"Musicians must make music, artists must paint, poets must write if they are to be ultimately at peace with themselves. What human beings can be, they must be. They must be true to their own nature." -Abraham Maslow.

Almost a week ago, Wendy and I are watching "Being John Malkovich" and John Cusack is doing a... (I can't get over Wendy's brain. I have no idea what the play was. Wendy walks in as I'm typing this, a fresh can of her eternally grafted Diet Coke in her right hand.)

"Wendy, what was the play John Cusack was doing when he got punched?"

"Abelard and Heloise"

See? Who knows that? No one I know.

John Cusack is doing a puppet show of the famous love affair. The longing of the two puppet lovers gets a little, shall we say, heated, while a little girl watches. Her father turns around to see the puppets humping through a wall, calls John Cusack a bastard, punches him in the face and kicks over his puppet show.

John arrives home to his wife, the lovely (though not in this movie) Cameron Diaz, and she cries out with alarm-

"Oh John, not again! How did this happen?"

"I'm a puppeteer."

Of course he is.

What are you?

I'm a writer. Delays or no, I know my destiny.

I hope that most of you reading this will eventually know the peace that comes with knowing what you are. What you are supposed to do. What are you obsessed with. To know the thing that drives you. You have to do the thing you are obsessed with. You have to be who you are. It is a great feeling knowing what that is.

A Pig Leg in Paris

I have now been in Madrid for a little over a month. I have been doing computer Spanish lessons, have made up flashcards and have been playing just enough Magic to be able to write my two-hundred dollar a week column about it. Not a lot of money, but a good supplement to my savings for writing about a game I love to play.

This month we are heading to Paris. Wendy asked her childhood-and-still-best-friend Colette when a good time to visit her in Paris would be. She immediately said, "You have to come up this Wednesday; I'm having a big media party for work."

Colette's husband Mathieu is Wendy's boss, and Thursday is his birthday. He loves all things Spanish, especially *jamon Iberico*: A very special type of black-footed pig that is fed on acorns and its meat is cured for at least two years. It has been compared to Kobe beef for expense, health benefits, and the marbling of the meat. It is a Spanish delicacy and very expensive. Despite the price tag of a hundred dollars a pound, it is consumed voraciously by Spaniards daily.

When I first moved over here Wendy wanted to introduce me to it. We went to El Corte Ingles to select a grade and asked the butcher what he would recommend.

"What is the *jamon* for?"
"It's his first time tasting *jamon*."

You would have thought she told him it was for losing my virginity, which makes for an unpleasant image. He was solemn, yet happy. "Oh you are so lucky. I wish I was you, tasting *jamon* for the first time. It is the best food on the planet. You will love it I promise you. You must have the very best *jamon*. Take this beautiful woman, wait for the sun to start to go down, open a bottle of fine Rioja and savor every bite. Your first taste only comes once in a lifetime."

That night we sat on the terrace, sipped wine and I tried *jamon*. I didn't really get it. I didn't see what the big deal was. The second time it tasted a little better. There was a tickle in the back of my head like the glimmer of knowledge. The third time I had *jamon*, I

71

got it. I couldn't get enough of it. I now understood why Spaniards go so crazy for the stuff.

In Spanish class one day, our teacher Montse told the class her first *jamon* story. It was Christmas and she wrote a letter to Santa.

"Dear Santa, I have been a good girl all year and I only want one thing for Christmas: my very own *jamon*. I promise to leave hay under my bed for your hungry reindeer.

Love, Montse."

Christmas came and Montse got a bike and a Barbie and some new clothes and a few other toys. Her mother asked her at the end of the day "How was your Christmas Montse?"

"It was good Mama. I got a lot of things I wanted."

"You seem a little disappointed."

"Well, really I only asked for one thing and I didn't get it."

"Did you look under your bed?"

"No!" And rushing to her bed, Montse finds a whole detached back leg of a pig under it. How wonderful! A *jamon* all her own!

It is much cheaper if you buy an entire leg and carve it yourself. This requires a *jamonera* (which I now have) for holding the ham leg in place and a very sharp, thin, flexible knife, since *jamon* should be sliced razor thin. We keep a leg on our kitchen counter and it can last there for months.

We head down to the Museum of Ham (which is not a museum at all, but actually both a store and a restaurant chain in Spain) to buy a package of *jamon* for Mathieu. But on the way there, we see a butcher shop with an amazing deal on a whole leg.

"We should get one."

"Colette will kill me if I buy him a whole leg."

"Not for him. I was thinking we should get one for us."

We debate it for a bit but then continue on our way. When we get to the Museum of Ham, we find out their price on a kilo is a hundred and five Euros. Wendy ponders this for a while, and says, "We can't get him the whole leg... can we?"

"It will take him six months to eat a whole leg, and he doesn't have a *jamon*era."

"Well, Colette loves it too. And so do his parents."

"Oh! Well knowing that, maybe we should. Knowing Mathieu, he'll see it as an adventure finding a *jamonera* and a sharp knife and learning how to carve it."

"It just seems like a waste to just get one kilo when for a bit more we can get him a whole leg."

"And, it looks much more impressive to show up at the office with an entire pig leg with a little black foot than it does a little package of ham."

"Okay, let's go look at that deal again."

Twenty hours later, I have forgotten the leg while passing through airport security.

Luckily, I remember about a hundred yards away, frantically run back, and snatch it out of the security lady's hands that was about to cut into it and feed it to the salivating Spaniards around her demanding free *jamon* for all!

The plane ride is a blast - except for the fifteen screaming children and their wonderful parents. Every time the plane hits turbulence, the adults and children all scream like they are on a roller coaster. And every time they do, I want to spin around and shout ... never mind. Let's just say I'm still a little jumpy on flights and leave it at that.

In truth, that's the right way to raise your kids. If you get scared over silly things, then they also get scared over silly things and grow up that way. And who wants kids that are fraidy cats?

We land safely and at Customs, they randomly pull the guy in front of me and the guy behind me out of the line. Wendy grabs me and whispers urgently, "Keep walking. Keep walking!" My leg of ham has escaped detection. Run little pig! Run! While it's perfectly legal to bring a whole pig leg from one country in the European Union into another, that doesn't mean they might not ask you some questions about it. Or maybe confiscate it "for security reasons" such as a party, later that night, where it will be consumed for the safety of all.

We get on a bus, and they take the luggage and stow it beneath, but when I hand him the leg he just looks at me and shakes his head. Pig racist! I move to the door and ask the bus driver if the bus accepts pigs. He replies: "*Oui. En dépit de mes meilleurs efforts, je ne peux pas trouver une manière légale d'interdire des Américains de monter mon autobus."* (Yes. Despite my best efforts, I cannot find a legal way to forbid Americans to ride my bus.)

We are put up in a very nice hotel on the sixth floor, with a beautiful view of the Eiffel Tower.

It is early afternoon so Wendy and I grab some food before our night out at a little café on the corner right near our hotel. I order twelve escargot, which I have always loved, and they're amazing. The waiters are just as rude as you would imagine. We order, he asks a questions, Wendy repeats, and he goes "yeah, yeah, yeah," and walks off! Bread comes, and as usual, I don't have any. Then Wendy surprisingly unwraps some butter that comes with it and now I'm interested. Butter doesn't come with bread in Spain. It comes dry or with olive oil. Butter > olive oil.

I chow down eight of the snails and leave the rest for Wendy, but she only eats two. She's too involved with her goat cheese and tomato salad. We each get a glass of wine the size of a shot glass and pay seven Euros for it, which is about eight-fifty in American dollars. Not satisfied with my ten snails, and knowing I have a night of drinking with Mathieu ahead, I want to order a cheeseburger (which actually was on the menu) but our waiter has disappeared. While waiting for him to return, I check out the newsstand right in front of the restaurant - and yes, they sell porn. Magazines shrink-wrapped with porn DVDs. Ah, Paris, so different from the "land of the free."

In America, such magazines, if sold at all, have a white board in front of the naughty bits on the cover and never come with a DVD. At our local supermarket, they actually started putting the white boards over the fronts of "Cosmopolitan" and "Glamour." When I saw that, I immediately went to the service desk.

"I'd like to issue a complaint."

The high school senior who was working went into the back and got his boss. "Can I help you?"

"Yeah, I'd like to complain about your magazines. It offends me that you have white boards censoring women in perfectly acceptable clothing. It offends me that some people feel the human form, even clothed, is offensive."

"I'll make a note of it, sir."

Idiots.

Fight extremism in all its forms.

I stop reminiscing and go back to looking at magazines with blue movies bundled with them. While interesting, I don't see anything that looks couples-friendly and decide not to buy anything. Wait, what am I thinking, this is Paris.

Later, I check the TV Guide in the hotel.

Channel 2 – 12:00-12:30 - Dragonball Z

Channel 3 – 12:00-12:05 – An in-depth look at French military victories

Channel 4 – 12:00-1:00 – Bones

Channel 6 – 12:00-2:00 – National Geographic's Discovery

Channel 5 – 12:00-12:00 – Le Porno

We decide to cross the street and check out the other cafe. Their menu is in English and French and they have three eggs and fries for only nine Euros. That is quite a deal in Paris and I love eggs and fries. The waiter is similarly brisk and dismissive, but we do get our food and it is also delicious. Sated, we order another thimbleful of wine and people watch for a bit, noting that all the chairs at the cafes are on one side of the tables, all directed towards the street for just this purpose. There are no chairs positioned so someone is staring at the wall of the restaurant.

Mathieu is coming to pick me up at seven. He says be ready for a long night and bring condoms.

Wendy is going out with Colette to a business cocktail party. Mathieu picks me up on his scooter. It's been a long time since I've sat on the back seat of a motorcycle or scooter and it feels weird. It's even weirder as the evening progresses and he orders all my drinks and food for me, then insists on paying. I think I'm on my first man-date! Our first stop is a skyscraper called "Tour Montparnasse" everyone in Paris hates and refers to as "the eyesore." Criticism of the monolithic office building abounds.

It is said that the view from the top is the most beautiful in Paris, since it is the only place from which one cannot see the tower itself. A 2008 poll of editors on "Virtual Tourist" voted the building the second ugliest building in the world. It is surpassed only by City Hall in Boston, Massachusetts.

It does have fantastic views from the restaurant/bar at the top where we get a drink and a three hundred and sixty degree view of the city.

From there Mathieu takes me to a seafood restaurant and orders a towering cone of ice with different sea creatures embedded in and around it. I dip into some crab, mussels, shrimp and oysters. Then we're off on the scooter to his favorite bar. Mathieu is mad for rugby and this is a rugby bar with huge plasma TVs. We have a couple of drinks and then it's back to the hotel for me. I quickly fall into a deep sleep. Wendy falls on top of me at three a.m., tells me about her night, and then we sleep the sleep of the dead.

Wendy has to work in the morning and I play some Magic so I can write a column later and when she gets done we go exploring. Paris is everything you have heard. It is stereotypically so, a beautiful, amazing city, beautiful, stylish women and rude service. Since this is my first visit to Paris, we spend the day doing the usual touristy things. We walk over to the Eiffel Tower and look up at it. There is a beautiful park around the entire area and people have bottles of wine and there are picnics everywhere. Paris isn't as green as Madrid and some of the park is grass but a greater amount is sand.

Wendy and I don't have the patience for lines. Why stand in a line for two hours to see the top of the Eiffel tower when you can be at an outdoor café sipping wine and discussing your journey, the things you've seen and how much George Bush is destroying America and everything it stands for? We decline to stand in the massive line leading to the elevators up to the top of the tower and wander on.

For dinner we go to a restaurant that only serves steak *entrecote* and fries, and when I asked for ketchup for the fries the waitress responded *"Nevair!"* then stormed off and treated us rudely from then on. Apparently, the sauce for the *entrecote* is also to be used on the fries. Who knew?

We go for a walk along the Seine watching the tourist-packed boats floating along, countless young Parisians sitting along the cement shores practicing their music, couples having a bottle of wine and a picnic and a large gathering of youth having a party with a pick-up band of varied instruments.

It doesn't feel like an American city. Despite the late hour we never feel threatened or wary even as we walk along secluded tunnels on the shores of the Seine. Around eleven-thirty, Wendy steers me towards a walkway that will give us a nice view of the Eiffel Tower.

Naively, I am unaware that at midnight the tower becomes an enormous lightshow. A hundred meter tall Christmas tree on ecstasy. I have to make a phone call.

"Mom! It's Jamie! Your boring Vermont boy who hasn't left New England for twenty years and thought he could see it all from his living room television is walking along the Seine in Paris watching the Eiffel tower light up at midnight! You know what? You can't see it all from your living room!"

She is very happy for me. Well, envious but happy. She always wanted me to experience such things but I resisted for decades. When Marilyn and I took vacations in our twelve year marriage we took them in front of our computer screens. We attacked enemy realms, slew dragons and assaulted Darkness Falls; all from the same room in the same house for twelve years. And we loved it. I wanted nothing else until finally I grew tired of such things and, as mentioned before, got bored with it all.

This new chapter of my life is an awakening; a revelation; a rebirth.

The next day is more touristy stuff.

I have multiple geekasms.

Despite the fact that Madrid has shown me some amazing fantasy like architecture, certain sections of Paris are buried in it. We make our way towards a huge glass-mirrored building and I see a bridge covered in statues. Flanking one end are two towering columns with golden, rearing Pegasus at the top! On the right side of the bridge, a woman is holding the Pegasus's bridle and blowing a horn as if signaling the start of Ragnarok. At the top of the left hand column next to the Pegasus is another golden women, sword raised in defiance as if waiting to charge. Beneath the column on the left is a twenty foot statue of a queenly woman holding a golden scepter in one hand and a small golden angel in the other. Beneath the column on the right is a woman with a large cape draped around her with a cowl on her head but not covering her face. She is also seated and resting across her lap, held in one hand, is a golden sword that is easily twice the size of my body. The bridge itself from end to end is covered with statues, heads carved into the masonry, golden shells, other decorations and lamps. Across the bridge is the glass building and on top of that, a naked man (penis and all, this is Europe) appears to be riding a wave with two rearing horses on either side of him. Seriously, you have to be kidding me. This stuff only exists in novels; doesn't it?

How come none of my teachers ever told me there were multiple geekasms to be had in Europe?

The wonders continue. We find a five-story building where moss and plants completely cover the entire outside wall. It looks like a standing garden. I pose beneath two giants embedded in an archway, an arm laid over the center, looking down. I pose, looking up at them. They look down at me and I cannot help but hear them think "What do you want, puny mortal?" We visit Notre Dame and - it is too enormous for words. The hits just keep on coming. Colossal, elaborate fountains, pillars fifty meters tall topped with gods and goddesses, building fronts decorated as if temples to the gods. It is staggering. Just staggering.

That night we eat at Mathieu and Colette's and I show Mathieu how his new American barbeque grill works. We cook up some veggies and French sausage and marvel at the fact that classmates Wendy, Colette and I, from a tiny town in Vermont, now live in Europe.

We spent our last day walking under the Eiffel Tower, up the Champs-Elysees to the Arc de Triumphe (which again, is so awe-inspiring and massive no fantasy geek should ever miss it), back down to the Tuileries Gardens, and through to the Louvre. We only did a quick four-hour pass through the Louvre, but hit all the spots we thought we might find interesting. I found it the most interesting museum I had ever been to. Although the Mona Lisa gave us the exact reaction Colette said it would:

"It's dinky."

"That it is. Colette was right. That perfectly describes it."

After that, we were pretty beat, and it was time for more snails, pâté and wait out the time for our plane back to Madrid. Wendy suggests a little nook that Colette showed us the day before that looked very quiet. Our needs are simple: pâté, snails, and wine.

It has been wonderful and I sit in the sun and smile and sip my wine and eat my snails and wonder how I got so lucky.

The Grillmaster

Back in Madrid the cohabitation I going swimmingly, but I feel like doing more. Like cooking. Or attempting to cook. When I dropped forty pounds I used to cook a lot of lean steak and fish on the grill. Not much more than that. Here's how much I know how to cook. Wendy and I are at the grocery store today, and again they do not have any hard-boiled eggs like I have bought in the past. We have looked the last four times, and they are no longer stocked. This annoys me. I like to get up in the morning and have one packet of oatmeal and one hard-boiled egg. Good carbs. Good protein. Low calories.

"That's it! I'm just going to boil some eggs when we get home. I'll make them myself."

"Good idea. Then you can call your mom and tell her you learned how to cook."

So funny, that girl.

One of the things I can cook is steak on the grill. I have mastered that, being the voracious carnivore that I am. Of course, at home, I have a gas grill, and Wendy has a charcoal grill that she doesn't know how to use. She usually has one of the men at her parties run it. Today it's my turn. Actually, I guess now it's always my turn, so, I offer to make dinner and we get some nice steaks.

She has these little white charcoal starter briquettes that were used at her last barbeque in October. They come sixteen to a package and instructions say two are enough to start the fire. I was there for that, and they don't work very well. Stefan was working on getting those coals going for hours and I'm not going to let that happen. As a Leo, and a Man, my ego is large and fragile. I'm not going to be in charge of the grill, cooking for my woman for the first time, and have a fire that only "sort of" gets going.

I crack open these little briquettes and the clear wraps around them crumble in my hand. They are very old and very dried out. Well, these aren't going to last and they're probably not very good, since they're dry. I might as well use them up. I dump the half package of one into the bottom, then open up the other package of sixteen and dump those in too. Then I cover them with charcoal, and light it. In minutes, a five-foot column of flame is roaring over my head. I'm six feet tall. The grill is about two and a half feet tall. The flames from the grill are over my head.

Now that's a fire!

I pull the grill away from the side of the building. Sure, the building is stone, but this fire is roaring! I bet Rome went down something like this…

The column continues to burn at that height for fifteen minutes. When it finally dies down even a little bit, the charcoal is a nice perfect gray color. Just the way it's supposed to be after about an hour and a half of smoldering. I have broken the land speed record for getting charcoal gray and ready for cooking.

"Wendy, I need the steaks!"

"What, already?

Ten minutes later, the steaks are done and have come out perfectly. Wendy is walking around near me with the portable phone talking with her boss, when the front doorbell buzzes (We're on the fourth floor in a locked building.)

Wendy answers it since I don't speak Spanish well enough yet. "Yes?"

"Firemen. Let us in!"

"What? Why?"

"FIREMEN! OPEN THE DOOR!"

Wendy looks at me, startled - "Firemen are here."

Wendy buzzes them in and oddly, I start to chuckle. I lift the lid off the grill. The steaks are perfect and there's no flame. Let's hope this goes well.

Shortly, three men in heavy black suits are at our door, huffing and puffing. They are in full firefighting gear right down to the oxygen masks. One of them undoes his mask.

"Where's the fire?"

Wendy tells him. "There is no fire."

He walks in and looks around at the no smoke and no fire in the apartment.

"Two of your neighbors in different buildings called in a fire here…" He looks out onto the patio. "Oh, there it is."

He smiles and walks over to the grill. I open the lid for him and he peers down at my perfect steaks.

"Smells good," he says.

"Wendy, tell him we're sorry to make him come all the way up here, but we have extra for him and his men for their trouble."

She translates and he says, "That's very kind, but there isn't enough for everyone. There are more of us than you think." He goes over to the edge of the terrace and points down.

Below us are five fire trucks, two police cars, an ambulance, and an army of men, all with lights flashing and eager to get to work.

The three firemen chuckle, tell us it's no problem, just call them before we have another barbeque and everyone leaves.

We consider ourselves very lucky Wendy didn't get fined and I didn't get deported.

The steaks were delicious.

Rain, Spaniards, Bullfighting, and the Mafia

I got my article in late to the website I work for last week, then spent Tuesday simply playing Magic and reading replies. Tuesday was a lazy day. Wednesday was harder than a day of deer hunting.

I remember the days of getting up at four a.m., putting on layer after layer of clothes, slogging downstairs to a bowl of oatmeal and some coffee, and then walking into the woods by flashlight. The worst of those days were the days it was raining, sitting against a wet tree, with a wet ass, during autumn, with layer after layer of clothes getting consistently more and more soaked. Of course, we Wakefields take our deer hunting seriously. My father, brother and I get up before dawn, pack a lunch, and come in when the sun goes down. But that doesn't mean it isn't hard, and being a night person, I dreaded the mornings, especially the rainy mornings. Today was harder than a cold, rainy day of hunting.

Tickets went on sale for the San Isidro bullfighting festival in Madrid.

Wendy and I awake at eight, roll over, and sleep another hour. Then, with a fierce comic-book-hero-like determination, we arise, shower, dress, and make our way to the subway and eventually to the Plaza de Toros. Wendy explains on the way that last year the police handed out numbers. When your number came up, you got to buy your tickets. If they were doing forty people an hour, and your number was four hundred, you knew to come back ten hours after they started.

The reality that confronts us when we emerge from the subway is a line five hundred people long, snaking from the window, around the plaza and back again; and the depressing, shocking information that they are not doing numbers this year. If you want tickets, you stand in line. And they're breaking for lunch at one-thirty. Oh, and if you want to keep your place, you stand in line while all the windows are shut and no one moves. Had we known this, we would have woken up at five a.m. and stood in a much shorter line then.

Now we have no choice and join the Line from Hell. Wendy, as is her gift, immediately makes friends with the four old men ahead of us and starts talking about what's going on and how come they are not doing numbers this year?

"It's the Mafia," they reply. "They change it every year so you never know when to get here and they buy up all the tickets and sell them on the black market."

The line moves glacially slow. After an hour in which we have advanced ten feet, I advise Wendy to go home and get some work done and I'll hold our place. Unfortunately, her mobile phone is almost dead on its charge. I haven't brought mine, and she wants to have a way to contact me when I get close to the window or if I need her. So I head home to get my phone while she stands in line.

I get back to the apartment and grab my phone and more clothes since someone has opened the ancient cask of winter. It's colder in Madrid than in Vermont right now - and it is starting to rain. I also change shoes into something more suited to standing for nine hours. I check my phone charge. It has been plugged in for days. The screen is blank. Huh? What? Don't do this to me now, I need you to work!

I plug my phone back into the wall, and a little battery appears saying "Charging only." In very faint blue letters I can barely see.

Crap! Wendy is standing in the cold with four Diet Cokes in her bladder waiting for me to return, and I have a dead phone! The main purpose for me coming back here!

I let it charge for ten minutes and grab a book. Then I head out the door, back to the plaza to find a beautiful, shivering, tired, drenched Spanish girl with a full bladder, waiting to go home and get warm.

She hands me the umbrella, and I kiss her and tell her to go get warm. She asks about the phone and I tell her it is dead. I don't know what's going on with it. She decides to head home for a couple hours, charge both phones, get warm, and then come back.

She ducks into the subway and I start my vigil.

It starts to rain buckets five minutes later, with wind picking up and blowing rain sideways at me under the umbrella. Soon, there is a river flowing over my feet and since the rain is going sideways, my legs are soaked as well. I offer the meager shelter of my umbrella to the man in front of me with no hat, and a woman standing in the rain with a crutch and a cast on her foot. She looks up at me, smiles, says a bunch of things in Spanish I don't understand and huddles under the one-person umbrella with the two of us.

Twenty minutes go by and it shows no signs of letting up.

And then Wendy arrives.

Moving from the metro station to where I'm standing has soaked her hair and white shirt. Because, you know, I have the umbrella.

"I got half way home and found out your phone was turned off. It's got a full charge."

"Oh my God, I'm so sorry!"

"No problem. I'll call you soon" and she disappears into the rain.

In my defense, it's not my phone. It's her spare phone, and the instructions are all in Spanish. I've owned one cell phone in my entire life, and it didn't turn off unless you turned it off manually. This one apparently turns itself off after a period of inactivity. In other news, Wendy looks great in a wet T-shirt.

I return to my vigil. The rain lets up for a brief period and then becomes a torrential downpour again. This cycle repeats itself for two hours, and then something happens in the crowd.

One of the little old men Wendy was talking with at the beginning of the day starts yelling at people in another section of the line, apparently for letting too many people in. Security is summoned. Many people start yelling and I am not sure what is going on. I call Wendy at four-thirty and ask her to come down and explain it to me.

As usual, Spaniards (and, by default, most Europeans) *suck* at forming lines. It's really not that difficult a concept. If there is a line, you stand behind the last person in line. You don't stand next to them. You don't wander off and chat with a bunch of people, wander back, and stand next to random people who might or might not have been in front of you (since the line is four-people thick instead of one-person thick). For example, let's take the four grizzled old Spanish men. They were in front of us when Wendy and I arrived. Behind us was a man with a large yellow umbrella, who started talking with both them and Wendy. Soon he was beside them. Then he wandered off. Two of the men also wandered off and then came back to the first man, to stand beside him. The people in front of them were also of the same mindset. They started talking with the four men. Some of them wandered off, and then came back. One of the original three men came back and stood in front of the group of men to whom they'd started talking. The man with the large yellow umbrella came back and stood in front of him, and they all started talking.

This goes on all day. Soon the line is eight-people thick, and the men who were originally standing in front of me are now to the right of me and eight feet forward. Beside me is a woman I have never seen before. She seems to think she is ahead of me. I have no idea because the people I'm supposed to be behind have moved up twenty places. Sort of - because they are standing beside the line, and not actually in it. This is about the eleventy-billionth time this has happened to me in Europe.

Wendy shows up and checks out the story with the little old men. She explains that some people were letting their friends into line over and over again to buy tickets, so the back of the line wasn't moving even though the front was. One of the older gentleman we were originally beside had decided to become the hero of the people, and started making lots of accusations; like, "Mafia!" His friends backed him up. The woman behind me started yelling things to the crowd to instigate them even more. More security was called. People calmed down just before it looked like a riot was going to start. That's when I called Wendy.

When we finally get up to where we can observe the windows, we see people ignoring the two hundred person lines and just sneaking into the front of the queue. And security is looking the other way! Our group (including the woman behind us who was inciting earlier) keeps alerting security to thirty or forty people trying to sneak in over the next ninety minutes, and they are shooed away once security is forced to see what is happening. Eventually, we turn a corner and can no longer view all the windows and the shooing stops. The security talk amongst themselves - and on cell phones, as scalpers continue to dodge the line. Apparently our group is the only one willing to cause a fuss. I fully expect to wake up with a horse's head in my bed tomorrow.

One of the reasons it took so long is the rampant corruption of the bullring. Line cutters and scalpers are common and the police turn a blind eye. The windows probably serviced four thousand people in the time it took a line of seven hundred people to advance to me.

And it has always been this way. In his book "Iberia" James Michener states that, "I once had a full day in which to contemplate the sordidness of the bullring, for at eight one morning I reported to the box office in Seville to purchase a set of tickets for the *feria*. I was fourth in line. When the window opened, I was fourteenth, men connected with the racket having edged in ahead of me with the connivance of the police. At one o'clock when the window had been open for five hours, I was twelfth in line because all morning drifters had sidled up to the windows with bribes to the ticket sellers.

A policeman finally came up and said 'they prefer it if foreigners buy their tickets on the black market. You're expected to.'"

At eight o'clock when the window closed, Michener was fourth in line. He did end up getting tickets though because the policeman went to the window and explained they should sell him tickets because he was taking notes all day and might be a journalist.

The windows here are supposed to close at seven-thirty.

When the line moves ten feet an hour, and you guesstimate you are thirty feet away from the window, and you have three hours of time left to get your tickets, and you have been standing in the rain for six hours... you start to get a little tense. We finally get our tickets at 7:20 p.m. I have been standing in the rain for nine hours.

It was harder than deer hunting because I didn't drink much in the morning for fear of having to pee all day long, and I didn't have much coffee for the same reason. I completely missed my afternoon coffee until Wendy got there after five. When she arrived, I'd had a cup of coffee and some oatmeal since waking. I went and got some coffee and a chocolate donut to sustain me for the last two hours.

But we got our tickets. Surprisingly, for almost every day we wanted.

The day after that was for recovery. Wendy had phone interviews with people in America and India. I drank hot toddies all day to try and warm my frozen soul. The day after that, we flew to Berlin.

Herding Cats and Riot Day in Berlin

Wendy has a group of Spanish girlfriends with whom she watches movies on Wednesdays. Said friends take trips together without their husbands, and this year's trip is to Berlin. Wendy and I are invited. Somehow the "no men" rule is suspended for me. We are invited late, so we take a separate plane but get to stay in the same hotel.

One of the things disconcerting about Paris was the number of Americans. We heard more English than French, and saw more overweight people than you see in a month in Madrid. Spaniards are a tiny people. I am a giant among men in Spain. In Berlin, we saw even more large people than in Paris. We saw more large people than in America, actually. I was not a giant among men there, that I can assure you.

The trouble with Berlin is that most of the city was destroyed in WWII and has been rebuilt. It looks a lot like a typical American city and lacks a lot of European charm and age, which is why my notes on Berlin are quite different and much more sparse than other places we have visited.

We walked along some of the remains of the Berlin Wall, saw the East Side Gallery and went into the Check Point Charlie Museum, a fascinating place, filled with stories about life before, during and after the wall. Stories of escapes, failed escapes and even devices used to escape. The museum has the homemade hot air balloon one family used to escape, and a car with a hollow hidden seat that smuggled people out.

Over the next five days we spend some time with the eleven women, but other days we just wandered around by ourselves. It was quite a mixture of heaven and hell for me.

Heaven — In a bar dancing, surrounded by eleven women.
Heaven — Finally eating wild boar. Something I have wanted to do since I was a child reading "Asterix and Obelix."
Hell — Eleven women speaking Spanish at once all through dinner when I don't understand it yet.

Heaven — Being called "Ali Baba," "The Sheik," and "The Man" for five days.

Heaven — Miraculously finding two van-cabs at night when all the women were cold and wanted to go home. They were talking amongst themselves and didn't notice our salvation. I hailing them, they are unoccupied, they both pull over and all the women start shouting "The Man! The Man!"

Hell — Herding cats through Berlin. Women are such gatherers. They're really not interested in going in a straight line to a destination but prefer looking down side streets, wandering into random shops, stopping in front of buildings to read plaques, going into bars for a drink. Proceeding directly to one place was almost unheard of with this group.

At one point, I am traveling with them on the subway through a tough part of town. There are lots of men and women with chains as clothing accessories and also lots of people holding large bottles of beer looking sullen and drunk. I am plotting that, if any of the women get unwanted attention, I will immediately proclaim that "All of these women are mine!" and demand that everyone "beat it!" Knowing that moments later I will be pummeled unconscious and the women will then rescue me and claim how gallant (and stupid) I was. That would have been funny. Sadly, nothing like that happened.

On our last day there, we visit the Berlin Zoo. When Wendy and I get there, there is already a long, wide line. We join the end of it. The next people to join the line stand beside us. I want to strangle them.

At the front of the line, it quickly devolves into chaos. Multiple windows open, with no rhyme or reason as to which person is next. After about seven minutes, Wendy sees no one being served at a window and says "Hold our place, I'm going to see if I can get tickets there."

The second she moves to the window, eight people follow her, leaving their place in line, and ignoring the people ahead of them. Behind me, I hear English.

"Should we join them?"

"I don't think so. We're too late now."

"It would only save five minutes anyway."

I turn around and, blissfully ignorant of where this nice middle-aged couple might be from and blurt out, "I find that Europeans don't do lines very well."

The woman turns to me. "No, they really don't. We find it maddening."

The gentleman addressed me "We can't complain though. It's worse where we're from. We have a saying: 'Second come, first served.'"

"Where are you from?"

"Africa"

"Ah, I'm American. They do lines very well there with ropes and security guards and signs and tasers for those who try to cut."

"Yes, we know. America is very organized. We go there sometimes just to regain our sanity."

I laugh and Wendy motions me forward. She has tickets. Wendy and I find the zoo to be "not great." Both of us have been to the San Diego Zoo in our childhood, and after that, nothing else can really compare. This isn't an awful zoo, but we feel the animals would enjoy more space.

May 1st is Riot Day in Berlin.

We come back from our day of tourism and see Beya (one of Wendy's Spanish friends we're here with) and her husband in the lobby. He has been with us the last few days visiting relatives in the area with her. We ask them about their day and they ask about ours and we notice they have their suitcases with them.

"Oh, we're leaving the hotel. Each year on this date there are riots in this area so we're moving a safer distance away. Like, outside the city."

How fascinating!

Wendy goes up to the desk clerk and asks about the impending riots. I swear this is the actual conversation, not embellished in any way:

"Breakfast? Oh yes, we will have breakfast right over there in the morning."

"No, no. Riots."

"Riots?"

"Yes, because there are demonstrations near here. We heard they sometimes riot in this area."

"Oh! No, no, no. That is just a street fair." He pauses and thinks for a minute. "But sometimes they get violent after midnight, but generally it's just a street fair."

"So, we'll be fine here?"

"Well, sometimes they come up here," he says. *And he punches his fist into his hand,* "and we fight, but generally it's just a street fair with music."

So of course, since we are insane, Wendy and I head into the thick of it that night.

It is just a street fair as far as we can tell. Just a block party that extends forever with bands playing, carnival games, little stands set up for mixed drinks and large cups of beer and grilled meat on a stick. You can't beat meat on a stick! The streets are packed like cattle on the way to slaughter. It is hard to make any headway through the crowds but we manage for three or four hours as light dwindles and finally disappears from the sky. Then things start getting lit on fire. Things in the street. We are guessing that cars are probably next. We have had a great time but make the judgment that things appear to be spiraling out of control and head back towards our hotel.

We are very wise.

As we are leaving, an army of police officers are descending on the area we were just in. Perhaps army is too strong a word, it was more like a platoon. We walked for ten minutes and didn't get to the end of the line of police walking five-wide into the mass of humanity we had just left.

As we check-out in the morning, I notice the papers have some very nice photos of burning trash and cars and police swinging batons.

Spaniards: The Good, the Bad and the Ugly

When I moved to Spain I expected to find that the people were similar to what I had grown up with. A little tanner, a little shorter, more black hair, and hopefully too smart to fall for the horrible fashion statement known as "sagging." But no, not only do their youth wear their pants halfway down their ass, the mullet is still big here too. This place is a fashion nightmare. On Blackwell's "Ten Worst Dressed" list this week, it says "1. Victoria Beckham. 2. Lindsay Lohan. 3. Spain."

Basically, I thought I was going to meet Americans that spoke another language.

Not so.

Spanish culture is shockingly different not only from American culture, but from most parts of Europe as well. In class, students from other parts of Europe express the same shock that I do about certain customs and habits Spaniards exhibit.

The good: Spaniards have a very close family life. It is not uncommon to see an entire Spanish family strolling through a park at eleven in the evening. Teenagers, newborns, grandparents, all out together for a stroll in cool night air at what would be a very late hour anywhere else in the world. And they are very physically affectionate. Mothers will walk hand in hand with a sixteen year old son or have an arm draped over their father, his arm around her waist. One of the peculiarities of the culture is that the children generally live at home until they get married, no matter how old they are. Once married, it's not uncommon for a couple to visit their parents every weekend. And well; they should, considering how much they owe them.

We were studying the family unit in Spain in my Spanish class. There is a photo of a happy family posing with this curious caption underneath it. "Juan (57) and his wife Maria (54) live in Madrid with their three children, Jose (31), Mary (27) and Pilar (24)."

Can you imagine? You know what will help you imagine? "Makin' babies." This is a common expression for Wendy and I when we go jogging through Temple de Diebold park in Madrid.

"Did you see the couple makin' babies over there?"

Over there could be a park bench, or a clump of bushes or the swings or just in the middle of the grass under a tree! When you both live at home with your parents, where else do you go at thirty-one years old to get some snuggle time with your date? Now, I'm not saying they're under a tree doing heavy petting or making love, but they are kissing and fondling each other as much as they can in public. And they do this for hours at a time. I really don't know how they do it without a release. We're not talking teenagers here.

Spaniards are also very proud of their culture and their language. If you are in a bar and ask about a dish, they will happily explain it to you. At the bullring, if the crowd starts to jeer, you can ask the guy next to you what's wrong and he will happily explain the long history of bullfighting and why this bull is awful or what this matador is doing wrong to illicit catcalls and protest whistling from the audience. Ask them about *jamon* and be prepared for a long discourse on the wonders and health benefits of this black footed pig.

Stamina – No one has stamina like a Spaniard. What they lack in peripheral vision, lack of awareness that there are other people in the world, tact and grace, they make up for in stamina. Spaniards can stay awake longer than a college student on Ritalin and Red Bull. They can, and do, regularly go out to the clubs until eight in the morning, go home to shower and then head to work. During the two hour lunch siesta, they will sleep in the park then go back to work, finish their shift and then call their friends to see where they are going next.

Not just for one day, but for weeks at a time! An American friend of mine, Kate, wrote to tell me: "Years ago, in Myrtle Beach, I worked with a group of Spanish kids who came to work for the summer. They worked two jobs from 8 a.m. to 11 p.m. and then went out dancing and drinking until 4 a.m. then they invited everyone to their place until 6 a.m. It was amazing and I never heard of them taking a day off from it."

I compared notes on this with my friend Peter Jensen whose son is married to a Spaniard. His story is identical to mine.

Then there are the *tapas*. They are the first thing Spaniards (or even people who have adapted to Spanish culture) want to show you. *Tapas* are the little snack that comes with each drink that you order. Sometimes, it's not just the *tapas*, but maybe a *racion* that is particularly good. *Racions* you have to pay a small fee for, but they are the food the little bar is famous for. Different bars specialize in different little quantities of food. So, you arrive, you get some sleep, and then it's time to see Spain. And by Spain, I mean, the bars.

You stop at one quaint little bar with a wall of wine behind the bar and ordered for you are *seta's tosta* which is a mushroom with a little alioli sauce on a little piece of toast. Delicious! And so is the wine! Then you are off to another restaurant where the specialty is *gambas al ajillo,* which is tiny shrimp fried in olive oil with a small red pepper and a lot of garlic. Oh, that's hot. Also delicious. But you need another beer to wash down that strong garlic and pepper. Then you're off to a new place that has mussels in a hot tomato sauce. Also amazing, and again, everyone gets a drink. Then to a bar that specializes in *bacalao* which is fried cod pieces that you eat with a toothpick. Just delectable, but a little salty, better have a beer with that. Hey, how far have we walked now? A mile? Three? What time is it? Not quite fortified yet, your hosts would like to hit just a few more tapas places and then, the discotheque! Which is so packed you can't even move, let alone dance. And the drinks are ten dollars apiece. Now THIS! This is living.

At three a.m. I fell asleep standing in a large, tightly packed room playing American pop and stayed there for two hours and never fell over.

Spaniards, and those who have lived here long enough, can go forever. They can drink from two in the afternoon to seven in the morning and then go to work. Large Russian men raised on copious amounts of vodka have been known to beg *"No mas. Por favor, no mas!"*

"No no, just one more place I have to show you. Okay, maybe two." And by two they mean five.

In Spain, it seems like there is a festival every three weeks. Added on top of that is the very special, and yet, still very common, *puente* which means "bridge" in Spanish. What's a *puente* you ask?

Well, consider this: have you noticed in the States that almost all of our holidays are one day long, and sometimes you don't even get the day off? July 4th. Labor Day. Halloween. Martin Luther King Day. New Year's Day. Two days out of the year, (Thanksgiving and

Christmas) you will probably (not guaranteed) get two days off in a row. Woo Hoo! Lucky you!

There's a reason we're the most medicated country in the world.

Spaniards would riot and burn all of Spain to the ground if they got as few days off as Americans.

Many holidays in Spain last two days, some last three. And they don't move holidays depending on what day it falls on to maximize the work week. No. If a holiday falls on Thursday, then they have a four day weekend. A *puente*. If no one is coming to work on Thursday, why would you work on Friday? Wouldn't a four day weekend be much better? Of course it would, so everyone takes one. And they don't use vacation days either. This is a *puente*. The business just doesn't open. The best *puente*s are when there is a holiday on Tuesday and Thursday. Free week off for everyone! (Well, everyone except the service industry which is always the worst industry in the world to work for because of this. Really, who wants to work on Christmas?)

Madrid's Second of May is similar to Mexico's "Cinco de Mayo" or Fifth of May, celebrating the kicking of Napoleon's ass. Now, the second of May was actually on a Friday, but for some reason, Thursday and Friday were both holidays. Maybe they were off on Thursday so they could get ready for the holiday. I don't know. School was closed both days. My private conversation teacher asked if we could have class on Tuesday instead of Wednesday because she was leaving early Wednesday morning to beat the traffic out of the city. See if you can follow this:

Friday is the actual holiday.

Thursday is sort of a gimme.

Most businesses closed by noon Wednesday because the next two days were holidays. My Spanish teacher left early Wednesday morning to get out of the city before the traffic started to get bad.

In America, you might not get Friday off (the only real actual holiday) but in Madrid, you leave work at noon Wednesday.

Can you see the draw to live in a country that doesn't care about nudity, gives you five weeks of vacation the day you sign up for a job, allows you to have a beer at lunch break, has health care for everyone, and leaves for a Friday vacation at noon on Wednesday?

They're kind of relaxed here.

The flip side of that is, well, they're kind of relaxed here.

How is that bad, you ask?

Well, they don't post hours on the doors of business. That way, they can open and close whenever they want, and often do. I've tried the door of McDonalds at ten in the morning and found it closed. While searching for a time they opened, nothing could be found on the doors or windows. Wendy and I once waited, starving, until nine p.m. (their normal opening hour) to visit our favorite paella place only to be turned away at the door. "Why?"

"Well, business was so brisk in the afternoon we just decided to stay open through lunch and close early."

Great!

Bastards. We're starving!

Waiters don't live on tips, so it makes dining much more relaxed. Rather than up-sell you, if you ask, they will even tell you that yes, fat ass, you have ordered too much food for the amount of people you have. And they love it when you dawdle at the table because they are not in a rush to turn it. If you leave then they have to do more work on the next people that come in. They have to get them menus, then take orders, then get drinks, and then the orders are ready... so much bother! It's really much better if you just sit and have another glass of wine; on the house, of course.

Of course, the downside of that is - waiters don't live on tips. I've been ignored for an hour and found my waiter sitting on a stool watching TV when I finally tracked him down. Of course, ignored would be too strong a word. Ignored is what would be happening in America. In Spain, it's just the culture. The attitude is, hey, you were having wine with a pretty woman. If you wanted something else, come in and find me. No problem. Glad to help, just ask.

Eventually the waiter will come back and ask if you are finished and would like anything else, dessert perhaps, or some coffee? No, nothing else, we're totally stuffed, thanks.

Plates are cleared. You have made it plain that you want nothing else.

The waiter disappears and the bill never comes. No matter how many times we go out to eat this always astounds me. Again, it is the relaxed culture. It's rude to present the bill to the customer after he's eaten. They don't want to rush you out. You have to specifically ask for the bill or it won't come. You could sit until doomsday.

When you do remember that you have to ask for the bill after a meal, the waiter will offer you an after-dinner drink. There is a select group of traditional after dinner drinks that you can ask for, and are normally free. I assume as a gesture of "Hey, thanks for eating here." I prefer *licor de hierba* which is a green drink that has a nice minty taste to it.

They bring you a little shot glass and the bottle.

That's right, the whole bottle.

Have as much as you want. Sit as long as you like.

In relation to that is the completely casual way checks are handled. There are some places you ask for the bill and they have one ready and it is correct. In others they have completely forgotten many items and you have to remind them you had more than is on the bill. Usually they will respond with "oh well, it's a gift of the house." Still others you will be in a crowded bar, order multiple things, ask to pay for the bill and the guy behind the bar will say "Sure, what did you have?" (Please be honest, we find this so charming. Don't ruin it.)

With the good you have to accept the bad.

Madrileños are notoriously rude, have no sense of time, walk as if permanently drunk, and speak with a mouth that would make a prison guard blush. They answer the phone with the equivalent of "Speak" or "Speak to me" or just "What?" When entering into a bar or restaurant it's not uncommon to be greeted with the literal translation of "What do you want?" which could be loosely translated as "What'll you have?" crossed with "Great, more customers to serve. Yay."

(Please note that I am differentiating between *Madrileños* and Spaniards because I have had much better experiences in the smaller towns and cities around Spain.)

In the states, when you are in kindergarten (that's German for "children's garden" you know) one of the first things you learn is how to line up, usually single file. Standing in line and knowing your place in line is very important. Cutting in line is very bad and can get your hand smacked or in some red states, killed.

As previously mentioned, forming a line is a foreign concept to most Spaniards. Watching Spaniards try to form a line reminds me of the story "The Last Little Duckling," which, if you haven't heard, goes something like this: A boy tended a flock of ducklings, and every day the ducks were let out to swim and eat. Every night the boy rounded up the ducks and put them back in their pen. The last little duck into the pen got a sharp rap on his ass with the boy's stick.

Well, one little duck found he was last and didn't want to get hit by the stick and instead hid and all night long had horrible, fearful adventures involving pimps and lesbian gangs. The next day he was last again, but this time he was happy to get spanked on the ass with a stick rather than be outside all night long.

I have always found this a very disturbing story even as a little boy. How is that fair getting hit with a stick for being last? Every day someone has got to be last! There's no way around it! One of those ducks is going to be last! I just think that little boy had a thing for duck ass.

I think this is the parable they teach children to live by in Spanish schools. "There's the bell! Everyone crowd through the door with no line! Don't be last or you'll get hit on the ass with a stick!"

"But Jaimito's in front of me. He was there first."

"Well shove by him! Pretend you didn't see him! Learn it and live it! Viva yo!"

Spanish people have a unique disposition concerning time and their place in the universe. It is best summed up by the phrase "Viva yo" which James Michener translates in "Iberia" as "Fuck you, go me."

In Spanish class one day, the teacher asked "Okay, you are on the metro and there are people in front of the door that you need to get by, what would you say?"

I chuckled softly. Other students looked around at each other wondering who would tell the truth first. Finally a girl from England spoke up: "You wouldn't say anything. You would shoulder your way to the front and just push people out of the way, saying nothing."

"Oh, that's not true."

The class all looked at each other, nodding. "Oh yeah, it is," we all agreed.

If there is a word for "excuse me" in Spanish, *Madrileños* are unaware of it.

Yesterday, Wendy and I went out for a run. Three people are taking up the entire sidewalk walking towards us as we run towards them. In America, I would slide behind Wendy, one of the women would either get closer to her friend or slide behind one of them and we would pass.

In Madrid, it's "Red rover, red rover, send Jamie right over!" None of them move in the slightest as we approach. It becomes a game of chicken.

Later in the run, there is a couple walking towards us arm in arm. As we approach them, they actually get wider, a space appearing between their bodies so they take up more room on the sidewalk as we approach, not less.

We went shopping two days ago and we have a cart, a large bag on two wheels that we put the groceries in and haul back to the apartment. As I am hauling the cart up the two foot wide ramp to the street, a family comes in. Two of the kids try to go down the narrow ramp as I am coming up it. As if expecting *me and my heavy cart*, to move out of their way! When I'm halfway up the ramp! What do they expect me to do, move over and drag my cart up the steps? I gave them my shoulder in response.

Even walking is an exercise in frustration. *Madrileños* rarely walk in a straight line, and all of them walk very slowly. It's the relaxed culture you see. Their way of walking is most likely healthier than an American way, which is to walk with purpose, in a straight line, eyes forward looking to navigate through the streets.

Not *Madrileños*. They walk at a leisurely pace everywhere they go. They also weave about on the sidewalk from side to side as if in a permanent state of inebriation. They have no awareness that anyone else in the world exists except them. Spaniards walk as if they are nine hundred years old; all of them, from the sixteen-year-olds to the mothers of small children to grandparents. Every single one of them ambles along at a speed of half a mile a decade and weaves to and fro along the sidewalk as if drunk and no one could possibly be trying to get by them. This works fine for other Spaniards since they all walk at the same snail's pace and no one ever tries to pass.

For us, it is a constant inward screaming of "I HAVE THINGS TO DO! MOVE! I'M RIGHT BEHIND YOU, NO DON'T

WEAVE LEFT; OKAY I'LL GO RIGHT... WHY ARE YOU NOW WEAVING RIGHT? WHAT ARE YOU DOING? WERE YOU BORN WITHOUT PERIPHERAL VISION AND DEAF?"

In the heart of a huge city, every Spaniard thinks he is alone. They will happily walk in front of you at a brisk pace, and then just stop to read a sign, completely oblivious to your presence causing you to lurch sideways to avoid running into them. They will stop in the middle of a major pedestrian thruway and chat as if they weren't surrounded by hundreds of people looking to get by. Wendy has had people smash into her, while standing in one place, and has them glare at her as if it were her fault for standing in their way! After they just crashed into her!

One night a few weeks ago, Wendy's cousin Molly and her daughter visited and we gave them directions to a favorite café. We arrived first and grabbed a table. They arrived shortly, we exchanged greetings and they sat. The next thing out of Molly's mouth was "Where did these people learn how to walk?"

Having never lived in a big city before, I didn't know if this was a city thing or maybe it's only town people that actually plot a route through a crowd. Wendy assures me that in Boston and New York that everyone plots a route as well. It's only the Spanish that seem to have no peripheral vision, no sense of anyone around them, no idea that they are awash in a sea of people and they are blocking traffic.

This is readily apparent at bullfights. There is barely enough room in the outer ring of the arena for people to press through and get to their seats. Despite this, there are hordes of people standing outside the beer and sandwich stands amiably chatting, smoking cigars and sipping whiskey. While chaos reigns around them.

And, as has been mentioned earlier – lines.

Wendy hits the restroom at the store and there is a line. Standing in front of her is a shrunken older woman with a cane. After a few minutes, another woman comes in, moves to the front of the line and stands there. The old woman with the cane immediately shuffles in front of her. Not afraid of confrontation, Wendy, well, confronts her.

"You know there's a line."

She looks Wendy up and down and snorts "How rude."

"I'm rude? Well, there's a line and you're behind us."

"I know that."

"Well you have to respect the line."

"I know that. But, I was uncomfortable standing back there so I moved up here."

As if being uncomfortable "in the back of the line" automatically justifies ignoring it. This is a perfect example of *Madrileños* logic.

At this point she turns to another woman who she also cut in front of and says "Can you believe her? My God."

The woman looks at her like she's insane and wants nothing to do with this.

Wendy moves in front of her and says the most insulting thing you can say if you are in Ecuador (which we're not, but Wendy spent 18 months there and figures a lot of what works there, works here.): "Okay, now that is just badly raised."

Today is errand day. The first place we stop is the Spanish equivalent of Kinko's, a tiny little shop where Wendy frequently does business presentation bindings and copies. Today, we simply need to copy the front page of our passport. We'll keep the copies in a drawer at the apartment and if we ever lose our passports they are much easier to replace by showing them the photocopies of the previous one.

There are five people ahead of us when we get inside but the line is moving swiftly. About two minutes before it is our turn, a middle aged man comes in who looks to be in quite a hurry. He is edgy, eyes shifting side to side, eager for attention.

And he knows we are in front of him.

Wendy is very aware of the man in the suit. Luckily, so is the person helping people and breezes right by him and approaches Wendy to help her. We get our copies and head out.

"You know that guy was trying to go ahead of you, right?"

"Yeah, I saw him. And I was going to call him on it if he did."

"Yup and he would have pretended he thought you were already being helped."

"Or would have pretended he didn't see us. Or that maybe we just came in to get out of the heat and have a smoke."

Capea or How to Eat Dirt and Like It

Come May we have settled into living together very well. Wendy works on her contracts and trains some new interns while I work on my writing and Spanish. We attend many bullfights and become best friends with Lena and Stefan. Lena is a tiny Cuban woman who works for Middlebury College and has been in the United States since she was five, but now works eleven months out of the year in Madrid. Her boyfriend (and eventual husband) Stefan, is a large German engineer with an endlessly jolly disposition and quick wit. They are both fluent in English but Stefan has some trouble when the conversations get heated and we start talking very fast and over each other. We have barbeques and picnics and visit small Spanish towns together on some weekends.

One Saturday I fought a bull. And by bull, I mean cow. And by cow, I mean small female calf.

My Spanish teacher Montse shares my love of bullfighting, so she knew I would be interested in going to a *capea*. (Montse is actually short for Montserrat. She says her parents are crazy. They named her after a mountain range.) A *capea* is a bullfight for people who have no experience fighting bulls, but would like a taste of it. Female calves are used and the rancher will watch them to check their spirit. Cowardly females are not bred to the magnificent fighting bulls of Spain.

Each year this particular *capea* is put on by Montse's friends to raise money to go to the San Fermin festival in Pamplona, better known as "The Running of the Bulls." It's not just a *capea* though; it's also a cook-out, open bar and all-day party. Montse gets us an invite and I purchase the tickets. She reminds me multiple times we need to wear white and should be there at eleven forty-five because the buses leave at noon- which in Spain means the buses could conceivable leave by one or possibly even two.)

We arrive at the bus stop in plenty of time and find a group of Spaniards dressed in white and ask if they are there for the *capea*. Greetings and cheek kisses all around. Then one of our new acquaintances decides that it's boring waiting for the buses and we

101

should all go to a bar for a beer. And away we went. A dozen of us crowd into a little café and everyone gets a beer at eleven-thirty in the morning. Ah, Spain.

The buses eventually arrive, we are allowed to board, and then the time slips to twelve-thirty, then close to one. I am about to go insane waiting but we are finally off. It's a short thirty minute ride from Madrid to the ranch. The location is a farm, not much different from the ones I grew up with in Vermont. There are tarps up, a huge grill, picnic tables and three guys working behind a makeshift bar. The sun is blazing down upon us, but we came prepared. We have hats, sandals, sunscreen and sunglasses. What we forgot to bring was bug spray and in minutes Wendy has me scratching her back.

"Is something biting me?"

I examine her back. "Not that I can see, sweetheart."

Five minutes later: "Something is definitely biting me."

Sure enough, we start to see tiny little black bugs that are all over both of us. Without bug spray, we resort to sunscreen to see if that will help and luckily it does. We make our way over to the makeshift bar and our choices are sangria and beer.

And the beer isn't working.

We get a couple Sangrias that are so filled with sugary punch that after half a cup my heart and mind are racing like a ten-year-old's after six bowls of "Captain Sugar Bomb" cereal. No more of that.

They announce the first bull (calf) is going to be let out and everyone makes their way up to the ring. There are bleachers that seat about fifty but those are full so we walk along the eight foot high, two foot wide wall and just sit there looking into the ring. The first bull is loosed.

She's bigger than I would have thought; about the size of a large deer, weighing maybe two hundred pounds. She has horns about six inches long and comes tearing into the ring exactly like the full-grown bulls we see in the Plaza de Toros in Madrid. She circles the ring rapidly, charging anything that moves. At this point, a couple guys dash across the ring towards one of four little walls of safety (barreras) evenly spaced around the ring. The bull charges them as they run and they duck behind a barrera before getting caught.

After watching a few people dash by her as if playing tag, they finally bring out a capote and someone does a few passes. Eventually the calf catches him square in the midsection and to steady himself he grabs the bull's horns and holds onto the head as she bucks and throws and people come running in to distract the bull.

Having watched dozens of bullfights, I can only think, "I can do better than that."

I make my way down to the ring but am unable to get the *capote* from anyone. I reach for it once when it goes by me and the guy tells me "you can't have this one." Since this is my first *capea*, I'm not sure what I'm supposed to do here. I'm not fluent enough in Spanish so I don't know how to ask or why I can't have the one that just passed me. And now the bull is getting tired.

An end to this bull is called so a guy shoots it and we throw it on the barbeque.

I'm totally kidding. None of the animals were harmed in the slightest.

The bull is let out of the ring and we all file back down into the picnic area for paella.

Paella is one of the most varied dishes I've ever had. Bad paella is not like bad pizza. It is just not good. Everywhere we go paella is different. Sure, the basic concept is the same, but how much saffron you add or how much chicken or how well done the rice is changes everything. Some places even add a tomato paste that we don't like. Today's paella is great. It is not the best we've ever had, but for being cooked outside over a grill, it is very good. The rice is done correctly; it is rich in saffron and full of peppers, chicken and a little seafood.

We stand around and talk for a few hours, and by "we," I mean Wendy, because I'm only understanding about every third word. Imagine a cocktail party where you know three people out of a hundred and you don't speak the language. Then we are informed a new bull is going to be let out so we make our way back up to the ring.

I have no desire to play tag and hide behind walls. This time I am determined to snag a *capote* and this time I do. Now I can finally see if I have learned anything by watching hundreds of hours of bullfights. I am determined to plant my feet and not move. Finally the bull sees me and charges. Honestly, my first pass...

It was beautiful.

The bull came so close to my body that his horn grazed my right knee, hard, but it didn't move my feet. I remained planted and wasn't knocked off balance. My second pass...

Face plant.

The bull ignored the cape, took me in the knees like a linebacker and I went right over his back and face first into the dirt, my teeth actually sinking into the soil. Around me, everyone is distracting the bull as I struggle to get to my feet and I spit out the dirt.

Let's try that again.

Success. Success again. Horn to the knee but I don't fall over. Success.

After a dozen more passes, I'm tired but I've learned a lot. Bullfighting is different than I imagined. I always thought you waved the cape in front of the bull, and led him to one side of you or another. It didn't seem to work that way for me. You have to watch his eyes. He is focused on smashing into the cape at a particular point and you have to see where he is aiming and then swing the cape in that direction. Sometimes, I had to move my feet.

But I think I did pretty well and I am very happy. I earned some bruises but learned a lot and when my arms got tired of holding up the ten-pound cape, I handed it to someone else and ascended the stairs to the bleachers.

I receive a few nice comments. Wendy says I was great; the best one yet. Montse claims I was better than the Spaniards and really showed them how to do it. Awesome!

This bull is retired and another is brought out. I don't see an opportunity to grab the *capote* again and just sit on the wall with Wendy. Actually, I am tired and after a bit I lie down on the wall while Wendy watches and chats with her new stalker; a thin young guy with big ears, big teeth and googly eyes. He is a nice guy who attaches himself to us for the rest of the night trying to figure out what we want next and fetching it for us. He tries speaking English to me many times but I don't have a clue what he is trying to say. He is able to get me beer though, so I let him chat up my girlfriend.

After those two bulls, dinner is served. There is an assortment of barbecued meats served with the hard, thick Spanish bread that always tastes like a solid bag of flour. I pile it high with meat as it does function well as a plate.

We spend some time talking and Montse introduces me to more people. The resident retired bullfighter gives me some tips. The guy who wouldn't give me the *capote* explains that his wife bought this one for him and it costs three hundred Euros so only he uses it.

At this point, about fifty percent of the people are completely smashed. Another thirty percent are well on their way. Wendy, me, Montse and her husband are part of the small percentage that isn't well on their way to a hangover. Wine battles start and for the next couple of hours people are going to the bar to get a drink just to throw it on someone. It's not an all out free for all, but pretty close. We are standing in the center of the turmoil but are able to remain unscathed with a little quick footwork. Wendy gets splashed a little bit and I think I'm the only one not touched by something sticky.

Then Montse pours a liter of sangria down my back.

A couple hours after that the first bus is headed back to Madrid and another bull is let out. Wendy and I decline the bus because I want to try another bull. I must win the crowd. I must do even better this time.

I make my way down to the ring right at the beginning because I want a fresh bull. When they get tired the charges aren't as impressive. The guy whose wife bought him his *capote* hands it to me and gives me thumbs up. Taking what I learned from the previous attempt, it goes even better this time. I shake the cape at the bull from across the ring. I keep my feet planted. I add as many flourishes and passes as I can remember from my extensive viewing. I don't get knocked over again, but I do take some more hits to my right knee, which is giving me a pronounced limp.

Soon (no lie) the crowd is shouting "Ole!" with every pass. Then they switch to "Torero! Torero!" chanting it so it comes out "To-rer-o! To-rer-o!" When I can no longer hold the cape out, I quit and head back into the stands. People are clapping me on the back, telling me "muy bueno!" and "torero!" and even "you have huge balls." Wendy and Montse are both effusive and I am glowing. Wendy tells me the people around her were amazed and loved it.

In reality, it wasn't that dangerous. No one is hurt the entire day, no matter how drunk they got. The animal is quickly pulled off by other people in the ring by distracting it with a *capote*, running by it, or even pulling its tail so it stops attacking a person that got thrown to the ground. On the other hand, you can't help but think; it is a hefty animal, charging you, with six inch pointy things. Imagine a two-hundred pound man with a Viking helmet charging you full tilt and hitting you in the groin.

At the end of the night Montse and her husband offer us a ride home so we don't have to take the bus. Thank God. (Montse tells me in class Monday that the crowd was so rowdy the bus driver had to ask them to be quiet and people were puking in the aisles.)

Wendy and I, on the other hand, are in a comfortable car chatting. We find out that Montse and her husband love American pop music and we listen to Van Halen's "Jump!", Gun's and Roses, Tears for Fears and yes, one of my favorites I'm not ashamed to admit it - Rick Astley all the way home. Which I think is much better than getting puked on.

Sunday I wake up with a serious limp. Wendy takes care of me all day, making me relax on the couch and keeps putting ice on my knee which is now swollen and purple.

It was well worth it.

Wedding in Provence

In late May, we fly to Provence to visit Colette and Mathieu.

We fly to Marseilles and rent a car for the hour long drive to Provence. As we drive along, I look out at the beautiful greenery, the coastline, the fields filled with vineyards and I come to a startling revelation: I have finally found a place on Earth more beautiful than Vermont. That place is Provence. I never thought I would type those words or feel that way, ever, but Provence is as green and unspoiled as Vermont.

We have a Hertz "Never Lost," which is actually a licensed Magellan GPS and it is a wonder. Do you appreciate the magical age we live in? A woman's voice directs us to the tiny town of Auron. Satellites, miles above us, are tracking our location to within meters. Side streets no bigger than a loaf of bread are mapped and tracked by a box no bigger than my fist.

"In 40 meters, turn left on Baguette 4."

I can't get over the countryside. It's like Vermont with an ocean view and fortified towns on the tops of large bluffs. It is like New England with ancient European buildings, large fields of wild poppies, and rows of grapes instead of corn and hundreds of kilometers of two-foot high stone walls. It is staggeringly beautiful.

Soon we are driving, in the dark, up a mountain pass barely large enough for our tiny Renault Elf to travel. It is likely a goat pass, or, more charitably, a hiking trail. I have no idea what we will do if another car shows up going in the opposite direction. This cannot possibly be the right way, and yet, it is.

Soon we arrive at the bed and breakfast that Wendy has found for us. The proprietor greets us at the gate, opening it for the Elf to drive through. He leads us out around the back to our room, and automatic lights turn on as we advance until we are at our door. Inside is a small apartment furnished with unique pictures, a large dresser, a bed with heavy comforters, a large bathroom, and a sitting room with a centuries-old couch. We walk outside to chat with our proprietor and look over a deep valley. There is a small courtyard with a couple of tables for sitting and drinking wine, or having a light lunch. There are dozens of strategically-placed flowers and plants around the yard and a full moon shining down on us. A light wind blows in from the north.

I'm not a sensitive guy. I have killed a living thing, gutted it in the woods and then pan-fried its heart in deer camp mere hours later. I have tried to choke a man unconscious in a submission wrestling tournament. I watch Ultimate Fighting every chance I get and cheer like a drunken European soccer fan. But tonight is almost too much to take. I am overwhelmed by this place. Wendy is clearly confused by my attitude. I am meditative and quiet and trying to explain what I feel, but I don't have the words. I do my best to allay her confusion.

"A part of me is sad that Marilyn will never have the revelations that I am having. That she never got a chance to see this. To be awed by this. To understand the beauty we never knew existed outside of the games we played. Another part of me is overwhelmed that I have led such a sheltered existence, and at one time would have happily died at home never knowing such sights existed in this world. Still another part of me is thankful and overjoyed that I have found such a passionate, amazing, intense, intelligent, beautiful woman with whom to share these things. A woman who expands my horizons to areas I never knew existed. To show me things I never would have seen. To push me, and make me never ask again 'Is this all there is?'"

She hugs me and tears stream down my face.

We open a bottle of wine and sit outside until it is too cold and then go inside and hide under the voluminous comforters of the extremely comfortable bed.

The next day we head to the most beautiful armpit of the world I have ever seen: our electronic female travel agent guiding us to spots unknown. How is it possible that Magellan has mapped dirt roads that lead to a dead-end five miles into the woods? How is that possible? How can there be an inn at the end of a five-mile dead-end dirt road and not have any signs posted pointing towards it so we at least know we are going the right way? How do they get any business?

We are here at this site for the first event of Mathieu's brother's multi-event wedding. It is a picnic and meet-and-greet attended by roughly fifty people. It is twelve-thirty, and everyone has a glass of wine in their hand. Wendy tells me she only knows a few people here, but they might remember her because of the speech she gave at Colette's wedding. Wendy thought the speech she made came off well.

This impression is made reality because soon we are swarmed with people shaking Wendy's hand, kissing her on the cheek, and hugging her. Everyone is commenting on the speech she gave as she introduces me to people, and soon I am kissing women on the cheek and shaking mens hands, all of whom tell me how lucky I am to have caught her. How brilliant and beautiful she is. What a great speech maker. How she single-handedly entertained an entire crowd. How masterful she is.

I tell them I know. I am very lucky. They pat me on the back and grab my shoulder and smile knowingly at me. There are kisses and wine everywhere.

I guess it was quite a speech!

Colette and Mathieu show up, and we chat for a bit and then take our seats for the meal. The two tables are what I would imagine in a Viking hall. Long, wooden and sturdy with benches on each side, perfect for a feast and the drinking of much wine. Trees surround them on both sides so we are shaded from the Provence sun.

Wendy asks me to explain to Colette that I don't eat *foie gras*, lamb or veal. I try to be a cruelty-free person in my eating habits, which is impossible in today's world, but I do what I can. I try not to eat baby animals and the thought of force-feeding a duck or a goose for days on end doesn't appeal to me.

Colette responds with, "I eat too much all the time. If someone were to track me down and kill me for my liver, I'd deserve it. Good for them, and bad for me for eating so much I couldn't run away." Then she stuffs more *foie gras* down her gullet and we all laugh.

Bruno pipes up, pointing "Ah, lunch is served!"

Behind us, a baby goat is descending the hill and approaching the table.

Bruno "And I shall name him, "Barbeque!"

Lunch is soon served and we gorge ourselves on cheese, potatoes, fluffy clouds of bread, platters of meat and jugs of wine and water.

That evening is another event at the stunning apartment of the groom's mother. It overlooks a town situated in a valley with a broad terrace for everyone to mingle and look out over the miles and miles of countryside. Wine and cheese are served and I do my best to hide from anyone who doesn't speak English.

The wedding is the next day and we have a little bit of panic when we can't find the church anywhere, park in a place we're not sure we're allowed to park and start looking down back alleys for hidden churches until we finally find it in a beautiful pedestrian square. The wedding is a typical Catholic service and everyone looks stunning, especially the bride, who is a former model. It ends after forty-five minutes, and then everyone has some time to themselves.

After the wedding, Wendy and I drive around the countryside, finally finding a quaint little town and stop for a drink at a little pizzeria. We are waiting for the reception to start, which, for some bizarre reason, is two and a half hours later. Three sixteen-year-olds and a twelve-year-old are playing a card game - and keep looking over at me in my pink shirt and Wendy in her beautiful dress and perfect makeup. Every now and then, they start laughing amongst themselves. Wendy wants me to pose for a picture, and they start laughing and trying to hide their pointing. I start plotting how I'm going to take out four kids at once. One with a kick to the midsection, one with a right cross, the other with a shoulder toss when he grabs me from behind - the twelve-year-old will run away at that point. It'll be all good.

A new young tough enters the picture, walking up to chat with the tanned young men in jeans and cut off T-shirts and homemade tattoos. Fantasies of beating up three kids and a child exit my mind when he air-kisses each one on the cheeks three times (kiss on the right, kiss on the left, kiss on the right again) and they respond with the same. As an American, at this time, thinking what I am thinking, this is about the most bizarre scene ever. It's all I can do not to burst out laughing. What was I thinking? This is a small town in France, not the Bronx in the seventies.

We go to the wedding reception and at one point, a shrunken, ancient woman comes up and asks Wendy and Colette to pose. She then whips out her cell phone and takes a picture.

I find out this is Maite. She is a ninety-one year old grandma on Mathieu's side who was in the French Resistance, married to a Jewish man who was in a concentration camp for five years, and she is now taking pictures with her cell phone. Are you kidding me? In case you don't understand my wonder, this generation has not exactly embraced technology. I have a hundred-and-two-year-old grandma who has never used a computer. She was spry until ninety-eight, walked a mile a day, all her faculties about her. Despite that, she has never used a computer, a cell phone, or even a fax machine. All of them confuse her terribly.

The reception is a beautiful thing held outside with a vineyard across the road. Waiters stroll around offering pate, shrimp and other nibbles before dinner. Moments before they call us in to dinner a station opens up that is frying *foie gras*. Wendy and Colette find it to be the most heavenly thing they have eaten in two days.

"Everyone inside, time to get dinner started" someone announces.

"No! No!" they both cry. "No! Let us just stay here and eat this. Go on without us!"

Eventually the cry cannot be ignored any longer and we file into an amazing building that reminds me of Hobbit architecture with earthen walls, rounded, fresco-covered ceilings and candles everywhere. Dinner was the most amazing wedding food I've ever had and then the dancing started and lasted until the wee hours of the night.

We get up the next morning and head to brunch, put on (again) by the bride's parents. We get there at one o'clock and again, every person there has a glass of wine in their hand. I think back over the last three days.

Day 1 – Picnic in the afternoon. Everyone drinking? Check.
Cocktail party in the evening. Everyone drinking? Check.

Day 2 – Wedding. Not many people drinking.
Wedding Reception that evening – Everyone drinking? Check.

Day 3 – Brunch – Everyone drinking? Check.

I get wine for myself, Wendy, Colette and Maite. I sit down and pull Wendy close to me so I can whisper "I just realized; I'm not an alcoholic, I'm just European!"

They Love It When You Try

I am, as the Spanish call it *"Estar de Rodriguez,"* which is a Spanish saying that means that I am home alone for the weekend without the wife or kids. Wendy has gone to Paris to meet with her evil overlords. It is amazing how fast I get bored when she is not around. I don't know why. I have books to read, games to play, UFC to watch, Spanish to learn. And we spend so much time together sometimes I wish I had a little more alone time to just relax. And then I find when I get that alone time, I'm bored. Such is life with an exciting woman.

I spend the day cruising around on the internet and gaming. At six that evening, El Corte Ingles brings our delivery of groceries and I put that away. I am starving because I last ate at mid-morning, and even then it was a lone re-heated hamburger. Strangely I decide to delay having any food until I can have paella. As an addict to paella, I decide I am going to eat across the street at our favorite rice place "Arrozal." But dinner in Spain starts at eight-thirty or even nine. There are very few restaurants open before nine. So, having made this decision, I'm stuck with an ever-building appetite and trying to stave off hunger until the appointed hour.

I head down to "Arrozal" at eight-thirty and the place is dark. I walk back across the street to a little bar and I read my new Bill Bryson book - "Neither Here nor There" which I love. Very amusing and I start to notice the man is also European, like me! About every two pages is a reference to alcohol, women he would like to sleep with, blow-up dolls, hookers or sex magazines. No wonder I love his writing so much. I decide my writing needs a bit more sex and alcohol in it.

At eight forty-five I decide I cannot take this anymore. If I can't get in, I'm just going to go home, heat up a pizza and then go to bed. I pay my bill, head across the street just as the surliest waitress in the place opens the door.

"Abierto?" I ask, which I'm pretty sure means "Open?" or "Opening?" or "For the love of God will you finally feed me?"

"Sí" says surly dwarf.

She lets me in and leads me to a table. She offers a menu but she knows I'm a regular and I tell her *"No necesito la carte. Quiesiera una paella mixto y vino tinto por favor?*" Which means: "I don't need the menu. May I have the mixed paella and red wine please?" She asks if I want a big or a little and I tell her a little, so she brings me a little bottle of wine. Which of course, I didn't want, I just wanted a little glass of wine. Of course, none of this is that smooth and she rolls her eyes at my broken Spanish when I don't immediately understand her.

I don't call her surly dwarf for nothing.

At this point in time, I am of the opinion that Spaniards are not that friendly. This opinion changes back and forth over the months but at this time, I hold this opinion. Wendy is of a different opinion, but that is because she is Wendy. Everyone loves Wendy. Bartenders remember her, waiters serve her before other people and the conversation she has with them is always full of laughs and smiles. I am of the opinion that this is because she is beautiful, witty, and talkative which are all qualities a man worships in a woman he can't have. Wendy believes it because that is the nature of Spaniards. I am pretty sure it is the nature of men when confronted with a beautiful woman who wants to talk to them.

For example – we have bought three legs of *jamon* from this little butcher shop on the corner. The first two we bought, Wendy was with me. The butcher got a nice big one out of the back, poked a stick into the center of it for us to smell and we assured him we think it is a good *jamon* and then he lovingly wrapped it up and gave it to us. The third time I bought the *jamon* by myself. He went in the back, came back out with an already wrapped up *jamon*, handed it to me without a word and took my money. No looking, no tasting, just take the *jamon*. I took it home and unwrapped it. It looked like it had been sitting in a bog for a week. Seriously, it was wet and green and it smelled bad. Luckily, the meat was still fine once I carved the outer skin and fat off.

Wendy tells me Spaniards don't care if you can't speak the language, they love it when you try. In my experience, if I *try* to speak the language they will *try* to screw me over.

Beautiful women just do not understand the society they live in. Everyone treats beautiful women well. Everyone loves a beautiful woman. They will go out of their way to see that a beautiful, friendly woman is happy. Everyone remembers a beautiful woman returning to their restaurant. When she smiles, bartenders fill her glass for free and chat her up like an old friend. They explain Spanish culture, they give her little pieces of tapas to taste and they remember her. And these women think that this is the norm! News flash: this isn't the norm! If a **guy** goes up to another **guy** and says "I would like to buy a *jamon*" in broken Spanish, the guy is going to go to the back room and find the oldest, moldiest, most pathetic piece of *jamon*, that he could *never* sell to someone that spoke Spanish well, and sell it to the gringo! Said gringo doesn't have the words to say "Shouldn't you kiss me before you try to fuck me? Why didn't you let me taste this *jamon* like you did last time when I had a beautiful Spanish speaking girl on my arm? Why are you trying to sell me a bog *jamon*?

Tonight is typical. With Wendy, they love us. Very friendly, great service, lots of checking on us to make sure everything is okay. Tonight – no Wendy and the experience is completely different. Bread comes twenty minutes after I sit down. No one comes over to say hello or greet me. My paella comes twenty minutes later and the bottom is nothing but burnt charred rice. I'm sure surly dwarf told them in the back to make sure to use up all the left over crap in my paella because the gringo won't know how to complain. So I've been waiting for hours for this place to open so I can have my favorite meal and it's nothing but burned rice, snout and tongue.

After I consume this horrible mass, I summon her over to me and she says *"Algo mas?"* which means "Something else?" and I say no. She disappears and I assume, since nothing is on my plate, my wine is gone, and I don't want anything else that the bill will come. Silly gringo!

I see her walking around the restaurant for twenty minutes and finally ask her over again, and being the gringo that I am, the only way I know how to ask for the bill is by saying *"Nos cobras por favor"* which means "charge us please." But, there is no us, there is only me. So I'm trying to figure out how to say "charge me," and stumble along for five minutes while she stands there, a slight grin barely hidden on the corner of her lips. Then she goes away and finally brings me the bill.

I left her a Euro.

Yeah, they love it when you try.

As if to prove me wrong, I went and got ice cream and the guy there was very pleasant, spoke some English and wanted me to tell him how to say "One scoop" in English. He actually did love it that I tried.

Addendum: I later discover that the bill doesn't come until you ask for it in all Spanish restaurants. This is because it is normal to linger at your table talking with friends and they are not in a rush to "turn the table" like they are in America. Wendy also noticed in the months to come that the ice scream guy has a crush on me and teases me about it incessantly.

Beggars Revisited

It is a typical work day. Wendy and I need to go to the electronics store, El Corte Ingles and a clothing store. When Wendy reaches a good place to stop work, we head out. We head down our usual streets and I spy a familiar figure: a rather large woman, resting against the wall of a church with a little cup. Her face is shrouded with a veil. She has a handmade sign that says "I need money for food, please help."

And I come to a sobering revelation.

You cannot save the beggars of Madrid by giving them money.

When I first came to Madrid, it was my first time living in the big city. I had to learn a lot of new things like taxis, the subway, getting groceries home without a car, street performers and beggars. Beggars took me the longest to learn. "Oh, they just need a helping hand. Look at this poor women sitting on cardboard with a cup out. She must be sixty years old, and cold. How sad. I will give her some money so she can buy some food."

"Look at that poor guy; sitting on his heels with just his hand out and a forlorn look on his face. Clearly he is a mentally ill person who has fallen through the cracks."

"That is an enormous homeless person. She doesn't look too bright but it's smart sitting outside a church so the pious will give her some change."

Of course there are many types of beggars. And by beggars I mean people who rely on the kindness of others and have no guarantee of income for the way they spend their time. Like the pleasant black guy standing outside the Corte Ingles handing out newspapers, opening doors for old women and even helping people lift their carts up the steps. Wendy tells me it's like a job, sort of. The papers are for sale for two dollars apiece but many people just give him loose change and don't take a paper. I don't know who the agency is that gives them the papers to sell, but I have never seen anyone but a black man selling them.

Other types would be street performers which come in all varieties, like the simple musicians that play in the street. Usually accordions, sometimes crystal glasses, sometimes whole bands with

116

accordion, flute, guitar and bad songs or even groups with violins, cellos and portable keyboards playing classical music. There are also the living statues, people in make-up and costumes who try to stand stock still, without blinking, until someone drops a coin in their cup and then they'll do a little flourish or a wave and allow a picture to be taken with them.

When I first came here I used to give money to all of them. The old woman by my dentist's office sitting on a chair with her hand open; the fat woman swaddled head to toe sitting by the church or the thin mentally ill guy with the glasses sitting on his heels and the nice black guy at the Corte Ingles. The living statues that covered themselves in clay and dirt and looked like unfinished sculptures and even, though I hated their music, the accordion players. My savings were fat, they needed money and it made me feel good to "help" them. One of my favorites was the little angel dressed all in white, face and hair also painted white, transparent wings on her back, little wand in her hand who stood near the palace. I would actually bring change along on our runs because the route went by her and I wanted to give her a little something.

And now I've been here long enough to have this realization. For one thing I now realize I'm living on a set amount of money that isn't going to last forever and... I'm giving it away to people. And then I start to realize those people don't need a hand up, they need me to keep supporting them forever. That black guy at the Corte Ingles? He's still there; selling papers, which I have never bought. Crazy guy? Still there. Large woman by the church? She's still there. Old lady sitting on a chair by my dentist? All of them are still there. And they will be there long after my savings are gone and I have become one of them.

And those musicians?

You're sitting outside on a nice spring day in the sun and they come along and play one song and then walk through the crowd with their hand out. It doesn't matter if you were in the middle of a nice conversation and their annoyingly loud (and bad) music called a halt to that for a few minutes. It doesn't matter that you hated the song they played. It doesn't matter that you're a captive audience; they just want some cash!

On top of that, Wendy and I have a terrace over two restaurants. Spaniards *love* to sit in the sun. On any sunny day the terraces in front of the restaurants will be packed with Spaniards and tourists and about once an hour musicians come along and play "I Did It My Way," "Tequila," "Rock Around The Clock" or "Hello Dolly." You know; all the Spanish classics.

"We're gonna rock! Around! The…"

"Wendy! Get the hose!"

Living statues are the same. The little angel still dresses all in white and stands on her white box in front of the palace but now she doesn't even hold a wand. Or smile. And her pose is just standing with her arms bent at the elbow with her hands curled into loose fists, fingers up. It's not too tough to hold that pose. She blinks a lot. She's become the saddest little angel. And after you see some amazing street performers, you start to realize the mud and dirt living statues really are just dirty people sitting on a box; with their eyes closed. It's not only lazy to be sitting but how much skill does it take to keep your eyes closed?

After awhile I have come to the inescapable conclusion that I can't support everyone. My beggar change has become much more discriminating.

We have statues like wind-blown guy that look as if he's fighting a storm, clothes starched back and umbrella inside-out looking like it's about to blow out of his hand who stands in an exhausting pose with eyes open. And tiny, beautiful women that sing opera in the streets and draw a circle of people around them because they have such talent. We have the old couple that not only plays the accordion in front of the palace but sing and sway back and forth, arms around each other looking like they still have the same amount of love for each other as they did on their wedding day. Those people still garner some change when we pass.

Deep Cleaning

In my quest to become the ultimate metrosexual I have not only replaced a gaping hole in the right side of my teeth with a bridge, bought new clothes (including a suit), and lost forty pounds, but I have also asked Wendy what she thinks of teeth whitening. She tells me about her dentist, and last week we had an appointment together. It was a bit cramped in the chair, but... never mind. Bad joke. She got a cleaning in one room while I got examined for the first time by her English dentist.

Yes, an English dentist, I know. Isn't that sort of like jumbo shrimp or a cheerful French waiter?

I meet my new dentist for the first time, a nice-looking man with perfect straight white teeth and an easy manner about him. He's very kind, explains everything that he's going to be doing and begins. He takes digital pictures of my teeth with a wand. Then he shows me high-res photos of them and explains what needs work and why. He takes me into another room and has me stand in the middle of a big machine. I grasp some handles and stand perfectly straight as a large machine rotates around my head taking a three-dimensional X-ray of my skull, then shows me the results. For the first time in my life I can see how far into my gums my teeth go. How crowded they are. How off-center my jaw is.

Okay, what the hell? In the middle of Spain I find the most advanced dentistry I've ever seen?

"On this side, we see the top of your jaw is compressed. There's not enough space where the joint meets your skull. And on this side, we see a more normal-looking quarter-inch space between the jaw and the skull. Do you know why that is?"

"Sure. Because before I had my bridge I did all my chewing with the left side of my mouth, so, for about five years one side of my mouth did all the work."

We go through X-rays and digital pictures and he informs me of the few problems that I have and how to make my teeth look better and how to go about the whitening. And then - get this - he offers me a 50% discount on the whitening if I let him use me as a "Before and After" picture for marketing.

While it's very nice to be saving three hundred dollars on my whitening, it's a little bit frightening to think that my teeth are so bad that I'm a "Before and After" picture. I mean, you have to be awful to get that distinction. Unless of course you're English, and then...

I'm so funny. *Si, no?*

This is the oddest Spanish expression I've learned. It's all the rage. Literally translated, it means "Yes. No." But in usage, it's more akin to "You agree, right?" or "Yeah, right?"

So, he says the first thing I need is a deep gum cleaning. Despite the fact that I see the dentist every six months for a cleaning and possible filling in "the colonies" my gums are in bad shape. A deep cleaning will help restore them.

A deep gum cleaning. Doesn't that sound pleasant? It sounds like a Magic card from the color Black: "Evil English Dentist: 3BB : Tap: Perform five points of deep gum cleaning damage to target American."

The horror.

So rather than play more games of Magic with my cool new forum-built deck, the next day, I have to go get tortured. I get up, shower, get dressed, and hop on the subway.

On the subway, sitting across from me in a light blue suit, is a Spanish gentleman of about sixty-five. Today is also his day for a deep cleaning.

Of his nostrils.

I couldn't believe it. On a packed subway, this guy is obliviously digging his finger into what looks like the deeper recesses of his brain. I stare in horror for about five minutes while he searches for what must be the lost Holy Grail and then I look away for fear of being too obvious. Well, that, and to hold on to my breakfast.

The following is the God's honest truth. I glance back after a few seconds of looking away, and the man is rubbing his lips with the same finger. As if applying lip balm.

Horrible!

Then he goes back to deep cleaning.

Of course, the whole time I'm thinking, "This is so going into the book."

I get off the metro and walk to the office, ignoring the old beggar woman still sitting on her chair, hand out, and a young and cute hygienist is waiting for me in the lobby when I come in.

"Hi, ready to get started?"

"Oh yes. You know how much I love a good deep gum cleaning."

She laughs.

I sit down in my little torture seat, and she straps my arms down with a vicious little smile.

Okay, I made that part up.

"My name is Sara, and I'll be your hygienist today."

"My name is Jamie and I'll be the patient screaming in pain today."

"Oh no, none of that" she laughs. "If you feel any pain or discomfort, just raise your hand and I'll stop."

"How about if I bite you instead?"

She giggles. "Promises, promises..."

Ah, we metrosexuals get all the girls.

"You have a bit of an accent" I tell her.

"Well, I'm Scottish and Spanish."

"Really? How do you stay sober?"

"Excuse me?"

"Well, I'm part Scottish and we aren't well known for being particularly sober. And Spanish culture amazes me. I'll go for a walk during Spanish lunch hour and see rows of businessmen with gigantic beers in front of them in the middle of the day. I went to the butcher the other day, and he was drinking a beer while slicing meat for a customer. This was at eleven in the morning. I passed two movers yesterday sitting on the back of their truck taking a beer break – at ten in the morning! We went to a bar last night and it was slow. The cook, the waiter, and the bartender were all chatting at the bar, each of them nursing a drink."

"Well, somehow I manage."

Sure thing. I'm still expecting to see her sip a beer between cleanings.

"Let's put these glasses on you."

"Oh good, construction goggles. I love to see those when I go to the dentist. Nothing I fear more than bits of teeth and tongue going into my eyes."

"Ha ha! No, no, it's just for the spray. We use some high-pressure water and fluoride that we spray on your teeth."

Whatever. I know it's for bits of teeth and tongue. She's not fooling anyone.

The cleaning goes without incident and then she makes me bite down on two trays full of concentrated fluoride for a full minute. While my teeth are soaking in this stuff and I'm unable to speak, she takes some fake teeth out and shows me the correct way to brush and floss them.

Halfway through I take the teeth out of her hand and bite her on the shoulder with them.

She giggles.

Wait, Wendy reads this...

Totally kidding. That never happened.

We finish up and I remark, "That wasn't so bad."

"Actually, that was just a standard cleaning. We have to do that before we do the deep gum cleaning next week."

Groan...

She smiles, hands me a glass of whiskey and tells me to rinse.

I knew it!

I head home to do some web research for Wendy. I have been working for her company for the past couple of weeks because she has a project due that she cannot complete by herself in the time allotted. I start some work and the doorbell rings. Okay, the new intern is here. I need to stop what I'm doing and train her on what we do. The job falls on me because I'm doing the grunt work. My incredibly brilliant girlfriend has to do the actual combing through of data, the calling to the companies to verify and glean additional information if possible, the writing up of facts that she determines are relevant, and then do a report to present to the client. Since the report is due next week, Wendy will be focusing on that. I'll be training the new intern on how we gather data and what we specifically need.

She is a very cute, very shy, twenty-one year old Albanian. She came yesterday for an interview with Wendy. After she left, Wendy asked me what I thought. First I should explain that I am a firm believer in two things.

1. That every human on the planet finds my Beautiful Wendy irresistible.

2. That every woman is two glasses of wine and a friendly backrub away from her first lesbian experience.

"She seems perfect: young; eager; intelligent. And did you see the way she looked at you?"

"Just stop."

"She was drooling looking at you."

"Stop. She's twelve years old."

I burst out laughing and Wendy rolls her eyes.

"I'm so funny, *si, no?*"

"Whatever you need to believe, sweetie. Did she have any questions?"

"Yeah, she wanted to know if you thought she was cute."

This is where you picture more eye-rolling and me laughing, because I think I'm so clever.

Risky Business in Galicia

It is late July and the Madrid heat is a hammer.

We have to do something to escape.

This weekend Wendy and I are heading to Santiago de Compostela for the July 25th Festival, *Día de la Patria Galega y Día del Apóstol Santiago* (Galicia Day and the Apostle St. James's Day). Santiago is in the very north-west corner of Spain, near the coast. The best seafood in Spain is on this corner of the map. And we do love our seafood.

Even the seafood in Spain is different and one more reason I love living on two continents. In the States, fish and seafood is usually breaded, battered, fried, and served with a heavy dipping sauce. In Spain, it is rare to find anything not lightly salted with a little olive oil. That's it. The taste of the meat is what matters, not the batter or the sauce of how long it was deep fried. Also the primary meats in Spain are *pulpo* (octopus, usually served on top of boiled potatoes and sprinkled with paprika) mussels served both hot or cold, *calamari* (squid rings usually lightly battered and fried with lemon) and *percebes* (barnacles.)

When we return to the states next week we'll be gorging ourselves on lobster, blue crab and fried clams with a ton of tartar sauce. None of which they serve here.

Variety truly is the spice of life.

Santiago (somehow Spanish for Saint James the Apostle) was named after the belief that Saint James was buried there. It is believed he came to the spot in the last years of his life and preached there until he died. Other legends suggest his body was shipped to the town after his death.

Regardless, his burial site was unknown until a shepherd saw a bright light above a field. He dug where the light shone the brightest and found the bones of Saint James. A church was built near this spot and an alter placed where the bones were found. When Moors were invading people prayed to the Saint for help, promising him a large tithe if the moors were expelled. The Moors were defeated and expelled and it was reported and believed, that Saint James was in the battle and fought on horseback, with a drawn sword. He was at the head of the troops, slaying moors by the dozens and earning the title *"Santiago Matamoros"* - Saint James the Moor-Slayer.

Known now as protector of Spain, Santiago has become a major Christian pilgrimage for over a thousand years. There are a vast number of people who visit it, every year, from France, Spain, Italy and other parts of Europe, many of them on foot. Depending on where you start on the pilgrimage known as "The Road to Santiago" the distance can exceed over five hundred miles (900 kilometers.)

We leave tonight on an overnight train and are very excited. Wendy has been buried at work and just finished a major project. I have been writing my ass off and struggling a little bit with anxiety this month and we both need the break. It's going to be day after day of seafood, historic buildings, wine and beach.

We are traveling by way of overnight train, something I have always wanted to do. Inspired by two movies, "North by Northwest" and "Risky Business," I am eagerly anticipating our ride to Santiago.

Wendy told me the sleeping compartments were small, but I literally laughed when I opened the door and stepped inside. I have closets bigger than this! Luckily the ceilings are high and there is space up top for the bags. I folded one of the beds away (which you need a key from one of the train attendants to open again) and that gave us a little more upper body space.

"You're going to sleep with me?"

"I always sleep with you."

"Beds are kind of small."

"They were small in college too, did that stop you?"

"Just saying."

"Dinner?"

"Sure."

Sadly there isn't much to see out the train. It is just getting dark as we get there and the windows show nothing but blackness. But we find the dining car (it was in a straight line, imagine that) order a bottle of wine and mull over what to share for dinner. We eventually settle on a bowl of seafood soup, a rare steak and pork medallions.

Train food is definitely not plane food, yet again something the railways in Europe have over flying. All three of our dishes taste like distilled essence of their original parts. Our seafood soup tastes like the bottom of the ocean and I mean that in the best way. It tastes like the sea and the most delicious creatures in it, all distilled into this little bowl. Our pork is succulent and rich in a pure flavor of pork like I haven't experienced in a long time, if ever. The steak tastes like a starving man would imagine it. It is almost better than real, tasting like someone had slain a free range cow that morning and slow roasted it all day and they just served the choicest, best part to us. We hope it is a sign of things to come, since one of the goals of this trip is to gorge ourselves on fine food all along the coast. And relax, which we both desperately need.

After a bottle of wine (and my "Risky Business" fantasy fulfilled) we quickly fall into a deep sleep.

Unfortunately the beds in a college dorm room are bigger than the beds on a train. My belly is also bigger than it was when I was in college. There's no air conditioning on this train, so within an hour of Wendy being held by a 98.6 degree blanket, we're sweltering, cramped and awake. And with no key, we have no way to get the other bed down. I sleep a lot better than Wendy does on the ride, but we're both still exhausted when the train pulls into the station just as the sun is coming up.

We take a taxi to "*Hostal de los Reys Catolicos*" (Hotel of the Catholic Kings) our parador (old Spanish castles that have been transformed into beautiful hotels) and thankfully, yes, we can check in this early. We make our way through the gardens and courtyards and passages of the castle and eventually to our room. I am disappointed to find that we have two twin beds pushed together but make no attempt to climb in with Wendy. We get into the softest beds I have felt since leaving my pillow top mattress in Vermont. The sheets are soft, the pillows are clouds and the air in the room is cool. Soon, we are both lying in a puddle of drool and snoring.

Three hours later finds us refreshed and ready to really start our day.

One of the very great things about Europe is they don't conserve water. I've never even seen a plunger because the tank dumps three gallons of water into the toilets when you flush. And the showers, like the one today, are not the stingy little drippings that we get in the States but more of a warm fire hose combined with a massage. You have to lean into it to maintain your balance. After sweating all night on the train, this shower makes me feel like a new man; a man that has been scrubbed and massaged by bristle brushes.

Wendy climbs in after me.

"Oh my God, this shower is great!"

Everything here is of the finest quality. We have enormous multi-layered curtains over the window that will completely block out the sun if we so desire. The sheets' thread count must be in the thousands, the bathroom is enormous and modern, and just getting to the room is a walk through history. Our window looks out into a courtyard with elegantly manicured hedges and a cupola in the center.

I am truly blessed.

We both need caffeine and head out into the street to look around and find a quaint little bar, Maria Castana, with a nice wooden bar, wooden tables, stone walls and some patrons dressed in period pieces. Wendy (because she knows everything) explains that they are *gaiteros*. One of them has a small bagpipe called a *"gaita"* and soon he starts to play. The music has a wonderful Celtic sound to it and a man joins him on a flute and a woman joins them with a tambourine and the bar erupts in music. The drunkest of the *gaiteros* (at noon, on a Wednesday) claps and shouts encouragement.

We have officially arrived.

Now that we've had coffee, it's time to sample some of the local fare. We've been advised by a friend to try a restaurant called *"Los Caracoles"* (The Snails) so we head there first. We get a couple glasses of the local favorite wine, a white called Alberino, look over the menu and decide to try both versions of snails they have for sale. Soon a dozen snails arrive at our table that have been drowned in a mixture of water, red wine, cheese, parsley and a slice of bacon.

1. The bacon was crap.
2. The sauce was crap.
3. The snails were crap.

Soon a second platter comes but this time in white wine. It doesn't help things. The bacon was mostly raw fat, the sauce was like water and the snails we tough from being overcooked. No Christmas card for the friend who recommended that place.

We decide to leave most of the meal and head off in search of better fare. It's clear we are near the coast and that's why we're here. Every restaurant's front face is an aquarium which has two different kinds of crab and two different kinds of lobster in it. In the window above the tank, shelves contain cockles, cigala, clams and platters of huge fish.

Risking another bad experience we follow our friend's advice to another restaurant and as she always does, Wendy asks for the waiter's recommendation.

"What is best here?"

He thinks for a minute "The waiter."

We laugh. So friendly here!

"Well, considering I don't see him on the menu and I don't know how much he costs, what's next best?"

He points to the *berberechos* and tells us they are excellent. As we will find out soon *berberechos* are cockles, which taste like a cross between a clam and a scallop. He also suggests *zamburinas* (a small scallop). This time, the friend's recommendation is spot on. The food here is excellent and as is the norm, served with just a hint of salt and olive oil and then grilled. Soon we've finished two plates and order another plate of *berberechos.*

We head back out into the street and see more people in period pieces and others dressed as Saint James with the traditional robe, scallop shell, gourde for water and a walking stick. The streets are just packed with wall to wall humans. As well as the festival going on, there is an endless parade of pilgrims/hikers moving towards their final destination: the cathedral. Eventually I can take no more of the press of humanity and request a reprieve.

We find a nice restaurant with tables on the street and decide to take up our favorite sport – people-watching. I order us a bottle of Alberino for our table rent and we watch the hikers pass us by. Some of them look they've been out on a day trip (probably true) and the others have the muscled legs and tanned, weathered skin of someone who walked the entire eight hundred kilometers.

Soon a tiny little old man sits down next to us. He pulls out an enormous cigar, starts to chomp on it and orders coffee and big snifter of brandy. We sit side by side for about an hour and then he gets up and takes his leave. Soon, a couple comes to sit next to us and they ask Wendy if she can move her bag. Only it is not Wendy's bag, it must be the little old man's who left five minutes ago. I grab the bag and go rushing off in the direction I thought he went. Luckily, he's still window shopping and has only walked about fifty yards up the hill when I catch up to him. I hand him the bag, he thanks me, I return to my table. When I return I find out he's also left a picture of a woman who we guess is his wife. Once again I go running up the street after him, and again, he's not much farther than the last place. I tap him on the shoulder and tell him "Tambien" (also) and hand him the picture.

There is disbelieving shock on his face. Apparently the picture is very important to him. He tells me thank you again and goes for his wallet. I decline and he yells after me something along the lines of hey, come back here. (My Spanish still isn't that good.) I keep walking and go back to the table. A few minutes later he comes ambling back down the street and he and Wendy start chatting. She translates for me. The picture is of his sister and is very important to him; much more important than the bag, which merely contains a new shirt. He insists on buying us something in thanks, but we still have wine so I'm at a loss as to what to do. He insists on buying us something again. Wendy finally allows him to buy her a piece of "Tarta de Santiago" (almond cake) but he won't be happy until I have something as well. I tell him I'll have a glass of the brandy he had earlier in hopes that that will please him. It does and he thanks us again and resumes his path home.

The brandy is not to my liking. When the old man is out of sight I ask the waiter to take it away and go back to my wine.

We go to sleep early and wake up very refreshed. Breakfast comes with the room so we go in search of the customary day-old muffins, toast and fruit. What we find instead is staggering. A breakfast fit for a king. A buffet of fried eggs on bread, bacon, *jamon*, fruit bowls, beer, bottled soda, toast, pineapple slices, ham, turkey, Spanish tortilla, frosted flakes, raisin bran, honey, mimosa's, and more.

We make our way back to the room and I take more notes on the hotel. We have to go through three courtyards to get back to our room, one with a fifteen foot ornate fountain, tall archways and a statue of a bear. Everything is made of granite which Galicia has in abundance. There are huge glass doors that look into a church on our way back to the room (yes, there is a church, in the hotel) and inside it there is a forty piece orchestra practicing. The scale of this place is staggering.

We make our way outside and are met with the same luck we have in Madrid. Construction. All of Spain seems to be being rebuilt right now. The most magnificent part of the cathedral is the "Porta Gloria," the front entrance of carvings. It is covered in scaffolding. We can see a stone pair of feet and that's it. Despite this, since we're here on a religious holiday, the church is packed with people. And, for the first time, there are actually visible priests seated in what looks like lemonade stands with seats to the side of them. People are seated or even kneeling to the side or front of the priest and they are either giving confession or getting advice, I don't know which; probably both. There are maybe eight priests on both sides of the church and some of them have little signs above their stand listing the languages they speak. One guy has a sign indicating he speaks **five** languages. The church itself is odd. The ceilings are not as tall as the other churches that we have seen nor as detailed. There is a sense of claustrophobia not just from the throngs of people but also from the church itself. While very large, there seems to be more pillars than in the other churches, creating a distinct lack of space.

I'm just not as impressed as I usually am when I enter an ancient cathedral. Of course, it's not the church's fault, the grandeur that I'm looking for is all hidden behind scaffolding at the moment.

We leave the church and make our way to a small plaza where the giants and the big heads are going to be dancing. Essentially, people in costumes with either large papier-maché heads or huge puppets supported on people's shoulders and the arms are manipulated by the man below. We brave the light rain and get a table at a little restaurant overlooking the plaza. Soon people fill in the spaces between the plaza and our table and the view is lost. We get up a couple of times to look at them dancing, but it is the usual show we have seen before. While entertaining, nothing we haven't seen a few times. Suddenly there is the sound of gunfire behind us.

This festival is all about tiny explosions. We look up and behind us, on the cathedral wall, a man is setting off armful after armful of bottle rockets into the air. He has assistants feeding him a steady stream and this goes on for a good half an hour of endless whirring rockets ascending into the air and hundreds of small explosions. We sip coffee and listen in wonder to the cacophony.

In the midst of all of this history, surrounded by the cathedral, the statues of Saint James, the pilgrims, the historic town – down in the center of the plaza is Mickey Mouse; gleefully prancing around on his big feet and making balloon swords for the kids.

The next day I can no longer resist the tanks of crab and lobster. For lunch we stop at a restaurant called Sexto (which actually means sixth in Spanish) and I pick out a *buey de mar* (A crab called ox of the sea) from the tank. Wendy orders us a bottle of Alberino to go with it, and right after the wine comes, the waiter brings out a crab, fully prepared and chilled; which is excellent for us, because I don't know how to eat a whole crab. I know how to eat the claws and the rest seems like entrails to me. Because of this, I've always considered crab a waste of money unless it was King Crab legs or meat in a can. This is perfect for us though. The entrails have all been taken out and anything worth eating inside the thorax has been returned to the shell. The claws are enormous, packed with meat and already cracked open. I devour the claws and then I rest. The waiter comes over and encourages us to try the roe in the shell.

"You must, it is the best part! In the kitchen, we will swirl a little wine in the shell and drink the whole thing."

I try a couple spoonfuls but, really, my opinion is unchanged. Wendy has more than me, and a fan of all things liver, loves it.

While it's great to have it all prepared and chilled for us, this is clearly not the crab I picked out of the tank. Perhaps they were just making sure I picked the right type of crab when I ordered? I don't know.

Later in the day I see something that makes me laugh out loud. A family is seated at a restaurant as we walk by. The waiter comes out holding a gigantic bogavante and asks a question. The father looks over the lobster and nods his head and the waiter heads back inside, ***dumping the lobster back into the tank*** at the entrance as he passes it.

We wander around the town some more looking at the different architecture, all granite and usually with a cockle shell or a statue of Saint James nearby.

The festival continues. The streets are packed with people in period pieces and many *gaitas*. There are women with tambourines and young men with drums. Every now and then music spontaneously breaks out in the streets and people stop and clap or join in with an instrument if they have one.

It is times like this that it is important to focus on the moment; especially for someone with panic disorder like me. I must remind myself to exist in the present. Think about this moment. Is this a good moment?

I find myself doing this exercise even when I am not stressed. Like right now.

Is this a good moment?

I am standing in the middle of the street. My belly is full of crab and wine. I have a slight glow from the wine. I am in a thousand year old town. The beautiful woman that I love is getting us two more glasses of wine. In front of me, a young, lively, beautiful girl is playing a tambourine. Across the street there are two men playing *gaitas* and near them is another man with a flute. There is a woman playing cockle shells as if they were castanets. The people streaming by us are all smiling and carrying flags. Spanish flags, Galician flags, Irish, Scottish and even Russian flags. A woman walks by me with a T-shirt that reads "I'm a virgin." And then in smaller letters in parenthesis beneath it, "This is an old shirt." There is a gnarled, bent old man who stands about four feet eleven inches tall and must be close to a hundred years old. He has borrowed drumsticks from a youth and as the young man stands there with the drum slung about his waist, the ancient man is grinning and beating the drum for all he is worth, easily keeping up with the beat and the other players. He is in heaven. Wendy comes back with wine and asks me if I'm okay, concerned about the crowds and my anxiety. I tell her I am fine.

Is this a good moment?

Smiling ear to ear I think "Hell yes."

There is a man on the street gently coaxing people to try his restaurant. They have a nice display in the window and I ask him some questions on the different kinds of lobster and he is very helpful and accommodating. We go inside and try out some razor clams, something you see very rarely in the states. Like all the food here, they come lightly seasoned in oil and grilled. There is no tartar sauce, no breading; served still in the shell. We find them delicious, a thick taste of clam and a nice texture.

I keep looking at the huge tank of lobsters in the window.

When I'm in the states, my favorite meal is lobster. In Madrid, such delicacies are too expensive to justify. Living in Vermont, I typically pay ten dollars a pound for lobster. In Madrid a lobster will run you upwards of fifty dollars a pound. Since we are now right near the coast, the price is a bit more reasonable and I can no longer resist. I choose a nice three pound *bogavante* and it must be a rare sight because the man sets it on the table, then the floor and people start taking pictures like we're at the zoo. Finally the poor thing is brought into the kitchen and slaughtered.

About twenty minutes go by and then our meal is brought out. I'm so used to boiled lobster I'm a little shocked (and shouldn't be) that this meal is split in half, lightly seasoned with oil and baked.

While tasty, it's not the same. Being baked, the meat is drier than I am used to when eating lobster. Also, a lot of the meat is stuck to the shells so we spend a lot of time sucking the meat off. While it does have a nice lobster-y taste, it doesn't fulfill my craving for boiled Maine lobster with drawn butter. Wendy's opinion is exactly the opposite. She loves the way it's prepared. For me, I'd say that the difference is similar to a micro-waved chicken frank compared to a New York street vendor dirty water beef hotdog.

Sated, we head back to the room for a nap.

We wake up at dinner time and my wise Wendy has made us reservations for the hotel dining room. Tonight is the night of the festivities. The plaza in front of our hotel will be packed with people waiting for the show. If we go out to eat, we'll have to fight our way through them, eat, fight our way back, and then hope the hotel terrace has enough room for us. This way, we eat here, walk out onto the terrace and watch the show.

The meal looks fantastic but we both pick at the multiple courses. We have eaten too much during the day and neither of us is hungry. The waiters are very concerned we don't like the food but we assure them everything is fine.

The culmination of the festival is unlike anything I have ever seen, and very hard to describe. I'll do my best though.

We emerge out of the hotel onto the hotel's terrace and seats are set up all along the side facing the festivities. We get some great seats and wait. In front of us, like sardines, is a sea of humanity, packing the plaza to capacity. Soon, the music starts.

The music is smooth and melodic and Celtic. It rises and falls and a fountain starts to rise and fall with the music. Fireworks start to launch from behind the cathedral and explode high above the plaza. Not the bottle rockets like earlier, but real, Fourth of July style fireworks of different colors and explosions. Now a projector comes on and beams artwork onto the rising and falling fountain. And then everything starts to pick up speed. There are more fireworks, the music gets even louder, the fountain shoots water two stories high.

133

This continues for a half an hour. It is a concert combined with an art show merged with fireworks and also a water show.

People keep screaming and "oohing" and "ahhing" all around us. It is a sensory explosion. I hug Wendy from behind to keep her warm and show my love for her because she shows me all these amazing things. All around us people are cheering and laughing with joy.

It is awe-inspiring

The next morning is mass in the cathedral. Wendy wants me to see it and I don't know what's coming. Neither of us are religious, only spiritual. We get there a good two hours before the service is about to start and all of the seats are taken, as well as any place to sit on the pillars or the ledges by the walls. It is standing room only and even then, that space is almost gone. Wendy and I find a spot in the entrance sitting on the steps.

Two hours go by and now my ass is very sore. Every free space in the church is filled with bodies. Police have cordoned off the church and only let in more people when someone leaves. Mass starts and it doesn't get any better. Time has lost all meaning to me at this point. Priests drone on. People sing. Someone gives a speech. My ass is sore. I keep getting jostled by random strangers. In front of me, two small Asian girls start playing with their pocket games.

Why in God's name did Wendy drag me to this?

At the end of the ceremony it all becomes clear.

A group of men in robes walks into the center of the church. They untie a massive rope from around a pillar and it has eight strands of smaller rope tied around the base. An enormous ornate silver urn is lowered from the ceiling. It is as tall as a man and maybe four times the circumference of an average built person. One of the men fills it with incense and gives it a little push.

At each apex of the swing, the men heave on the ropes until the urn is flying through the air, getting higher and higher in its arc. Soon the crowd is making little wonder noises. They continue to heave and soon the enormous urn is mere feet from touching the ceiling, and on the down swing, is flying close above the audiences head. The church is filled with incense. It is pretty spectacular and lasts for about ten minutes.

That was worth waiting for.

In the afternoon we drive down the coast to Baiona. But first Wendy asks if I want to drive north to Finisterre (Latin for "land's end") and the end of the world. In earlier times people believed that this part of Spain was the westernmost part of the world; after that - ocean and the abyss. The coastline leading up to Finisterre is hard to navigate and the site of many shipwrecks earning it the name "*Costa del Morte*" or "Coast of Death."

Yes, we're driving up the coast of death to see the end of the world. Doesn't that sound like fun?

Driving up there I am once again amazed by the beauty of Spain. So very like Vermont. Rampant commercialism hasn't hit Spain yet, so the countryside is virtually unspoiled by billboards. The land is green and full of life. The trees, a mix of pine, eucalyptus and chestnut, even look similar to the trees in Vermont. Also, every five miles is a new warning to watch out for deer. When we're not in gorgeous countryside, we're passing through one quaint little town after another, also like Vermont.

One stark difference is the windmills. Spain has embraced renewable energy and the mountains on our left are dotted with enormous windmills; dozens of them all along the mountains for miles and miles. I find them fascinating and not ugly at all. The further north we get, the more granite starts to peek through the fields until the land that once resembled Vermont now looks more like troll country. The mountains turn from a pleasant rolling green to solid rock. While there is still a lot of greenery, the fields become like rock gardens. Farming must be nearly impossible.

We finally make it to land's end and, wow, really not what I would have expected. The first thing that greets us is a donut van. Yes, it's the donut van at the end of the world. Next to that is a cheap trinkets and gift stand. Seashells, T-shirts (none of which say "Land's End" or "End of the World") and other assorted crap that has nothing to do with the location. Someone just thought they could sell random cheap stuff to tourists. Being American, I'm used to someone always exploiting the crap out of such places. If this was America there would be T-shirts and a bar and bumper stickers and tomahawks (because there are always tomahawks) and every place not cordoned off would be selling something. Here – A donut van and a garage sale.

We walk out on the well-maintained path to Land's End and look out over the vast ocean. The view is gorgeous and stunning with a large rock out in the middle of the sea to the east, the ocean going on forever to the west. The waves lap on the rocks so very far, far below us and despite a long row of cars in the parking lot, it's not very crowded. I crack open a beer and invite Wendy to share it with me at "Jamie's Bar at the End of the World." We are easily able to get some photos of just us sitting on the rocks with the coastline and vast ocean behind us.

For the end of the world, it's a little underwhelming, but very beautiful.

We make our way back down the coast and stop in at a couple small towns that look inviting and have some razor clams and oysters for lunch. I finally discover how to eat oysters. See, I like to chew my food. I like to experience the taste. That's why you chew. After chewing three oysters and not finding the taste or texture that appealing, I start to just swallow them whole without chewing and that works much better. There is much less taste, but honestly, a better taste. I slurp the last three with gusto and feel like a fool for not realizing this sooner. Everyone knows this, but it seems odd to just swallow.

As usual, the bill refuses to come. Our waiter has abandoned us to the wolves for about thirty minutes now. I go inside and find him chatting and tending bar and ask for the bill. Right then, a beer keg runs out on the beer that he is pouring. I go sit outside in the sun with Wendy and enjoy the scenery.

Ten minutes go by and still no bill. I go back inside and our waiter / bartender is nowhere to be found. I ask another waiter for the bill and he says "Oh yes, he knows. He's coming right out with it."

Sure he is. You know we're in Spain right?

Ten more minutes go by and Wendy decides to try her luck.

Fluent beautiful girls always have more pull than poorly speaking men and Wendy finally succeeds in getting the bill. Thirty minutes after the first time we asked for it.

We finally make it to Baiona and our next parador. Wendy has outdone herself this time. In Santiago, the beauty of the parador was all inside its vast interior. This parador is part of an enormous fort, with large grounds, a pool, a tennis court, and kilometer long path leading around it overlooking the sea. And the sea here is incredible, crashing mightily against the rocks below us. Sadly, again, we have two twin beds pushed against each other.

136

That night we watch a couple having wedding pictures taken. As usual, it is ridiculous. The photographer has the couple walking hand in hand on the grounds. Fine. Then he has him lifting her in his arms. Then he has the groom spin around with her in his arms. Then they are lying on the grass together. And now they are walking on top of the walls. Idiotic. As Wendy points out, these are all fake memories. The couple will never look back and think...

"Remember that time we were lying in the grass in our wedding outfits saying romantic things to each other?"

"No."

"Remember that time I was so filled with love for you I picked you up in my arms and spun around in a circle?"

"No."

And while all of this is going on, the guests are hanging out waiting for them to return. Wendy and I have talked about this a lot. There will be no pauses, no guests waiting for the next event, no fake pictures at our wedding.

We have dinner that night at the hotel's restaurant right on the sea. Supposedly lighter fare than what is served in the main dining room, we find the food excellent. We share a well seasoned hake and a rare steak with Wendy creating a bread holocaust on her side of the table. At one point she is pouring olive oil over her bread and it gets away from her creating a spot on the table cloth. In an effort to clean up the spot, she keeps dabbing her bread into it, which continues to fall apart, leaving crumbs and bread pieces all over the table. Undaunted, Wendy continues with the bread holocaust, moaning between bites.

"This bread is so good I want to take it home and sleep with it."

Eating with us tonight is the strangest array of people we've seen in a while. We are in full on people-watching mode and the show is grand. Entering shortly after us is a young woman with a slightly older man. She is crack-whore thin, oddly pretty, brown stringy hair almost down to her waist and wearing an outfit so *not* appropriate to this place. With her is a guy who has a gut like a beer barrel, stick thin legs, jowls, balding, dark sunglasses. Is he a pimp? A drug dealer maybe? They get up from the meal multiple times and go outside. Smoke? Cell phone? Crack? Not sure.

After we order, a couple from the wedding party comes in. They are very nicely dressed and young. The guy is athletic looking and handsome. The girl is pretty but painfully thin.

"That girl needs a hamburger worse than anyone I've ever seen," I tell Wendy.

"What do you think Skeletor will order here: a glass of water and a half a cracker?"

They order and soon a big plate of mussels comes to their table. Against our predictions, Skeletor actually eats a bunch of them. After that a plate of paella comes and Wendy quietly mimics her again "Oh no, I couldn't have any starch. I'll eat this delicious slice of lemon though."

And again she surprises us and digs right in.

"What do you bet when this is done she goes into the bathroom and hurls that all up?"

Across from us is a morose couple. They look like a long-suffering married couple that's not happy and on the outs. At one point the man buries his face in his hands for about thirty seconds then looks up at his companion. Wendy jokes again.

"Are you still here? I was hoping that when I looked up you would have left or magically turned into someone I actually wanted to have dinner with."

At one of the outside tables, a large party from the wedding is being entertained by a very drunk Jerry Maguire. This guy has an opinion on everything, stands up often, gestures wildly, keeps making toasts and gives lectures to his long suffering companions.

At the far end of the restaurant is one of the more frequent sights in Spain, a small Asian girl with her Spanish family. She is cuter than a button, well mannered and we remember her from our last parador where the family was also staying. They have clearly followed us to Baiona.

Even the waiters provide amusement. It is amazing how inefficient Spanish waiters are. Perhaps it is because they don't work for tips. But everywhere we go, they have, like, six waiters for four tables and they're running around like they're in the middle of an afternoon rush. What one waitress in America could handle with ease requires three Spanish waiters moving at top speed. They run back and forth with a look of dire concentration on their faces and you know they are thinking "Oh my God, so many people and everything's moving so fast and I can't keep up. Oh fuck I have to move faster. Oh my God, another deuce just came in, what will we do?"

The meal is excellent and Wendy's running commentary keeps me in stitches. But all things must come to an end. Except in Spain where the meal never ends. We ask for the bill.

Nothing.

We ask for the bill again.

Nothing.

We ask for the bill again.

And still we sit.

Finally, at the end of our ropes, we just get up and leave. Suddenly, the waiter remembers us and rushes over. "Wait, wait wait... would you like to charge this to your room?"

"Well, I've asked to charge it to the room three times now and you've been clearing, resetting tables and ignoring us.

"Oh, I thought you already asked for it?"

Which is an odd thing to say.

"Yes, I asked you and I asked the other waiter."

"Oh, we must have both thought the other had helped you."

Which again, is an odd thing to say. If you both thought the other had helped us, why did you dash after us as we were leaving the restaurant and all of a sudden know we hadn't been presented with a bill? But, whatever. We sign the bill and head to bed.

Across the bay, more bottle rockets explode in the air. Like they have been doing all day and like they did all day in Santiago. Clearly, Saint James is the Patron Saint of Explosions.

The morning is spent walking the path around the parador. The sea is at high tide and booms against the walls of past fort constructions about ten feet below us. About halfway around, we sit on one of the walls and just watch the sea for twenty minutes. It takes us about an hour to walk around the whole thing and it ends at a public beach. We grab a table and some soda and people watch for a bit. Almost all the patrons of the beach are sedately reading, making sand castles or sunbathing which provides little entertainment so we move along. Wendy, as she always does, wants to explore the back streets of Baiona and see the locals. And get some wine. There are advantages to having an Irish girlfriend.

We wander for a bit and find what looks like a fantastic restaurant right on the strip. The waitress is a cute and petite dirty blond who has a twinkle in her eye for Wendy (they all do) as she explains the menu and how long they are open (all day.) There is a stack of every manner of sea creature on ice by the front door. It is towering. They have a terrace. We will come back here for lunch.

We make our way through the town, every now and then Wendy dragging me down a back alley looking for the "real" Baiona. We find a side street that appears to be a second main street, but instead of cars, with people and restaurants. We pass one place I see the largest live lobster I have ever seen. It is about two feet long and must weigh in at over ten pounds. I get the feeling it is the restaurants pet or star attraction and I am proven right when a man appears at the door and says "Two for lunch? We have a table for you right over here."

"No thank you, just admiring your pet."

Another couple walks by "Two for lunch? Inside or out, we have room at both."

"No, thank you."

So not Spanish - most places we go by they barely want you to come in. More work for them, can't all you tourists just go away?

There are many differences between the center of Spain and the north of Spain. Like right now, at just after noon, everyone is sitting down to lunch. In Madrid, lunch starts at two in the afternoon and ends at five. Another is the type of wine. Here, everyone is drinking white. In Madrid, they almost never touch the stuff. It is red Rioja all the time. The bread here is delicious, light, fresh and fluffy and has a slightly darker tinge to it, almost as if it has a touch of wheat in it. In Madrid, the bread is hard, white, and tastes like a bag of flour.

We make our way into the maelstrom of people and finally find a suitable spot to sit and people watch. The crowds stream by. We order some wine. I go inside and use the restroom. I return to find a perplexed Wendy.

"I just saw the strangest thing. See that witch over there?"

Across the narrow street, about six feet away from us is a store with a two foot high witch doll next to the door, standing and holding a broom.

"This deranged child just came up and started jumping in front of the witch. Then he started yelling at it, then smashing his hands in front of its face as if he was trying to scare it. He did this the entire time you were in the bathroom."

"That is weird."

"Look! Look. Here he comes again."

And, just as she described, a child who must be damaged in some way runs up to the witch and starts clapping his hands in front of its face and then jumping away after each clap.

Finally, the child elicits a response. The witch suddenly starts to cackle and shake for thirty seconds. Ah. There is a sound sensor on the witch the child is trying to trigger. He's not deranged, just bad at clapping.

The crowds of Baiona stream past us. Skeletor's grandmother walks by, a rail thin sixty-five year old woman desperately trying to hold onto her youth but unwilling to give up smoking to do it. She has on a wrinkled tight black skirt over bony hips, badly applied make up over smoke damaged and aged skin and dyed blond hair. Next up are the "Basque terrorists." It's a running joke in our group of friends that whenever a person has awful hair, they must be Basque terrorists. Every time they arrest a Basque separatist and their picture is in the paper, they always have a mullet of some kind. The mullet is still big in Spain and comes in many varieties. There's the mullhawk which is a mohawk on top and a mullet trailing down your back. And of course there's the mullock which is short hair on top and sides with dreadlocks trailing down the back. We see a few of every variety this afternoon and Wendy cringes every time one passes by.

"Awful. Awful," she whispers while holding onto my arm.

We see a rare sight for Spain. A girl is completely wrecked and can barely walk. Her boyfriend has got his arm around her waist and one of her arms around his shoulders. She looks absolutely miserable and he is half dragging, half carrying her down the street. They get a table next to ours for a rest. He orders a beer and she gets some water and rests her head on the table.

The deranged child returns with other children and they all wildly slap their hands in front of the witch trying to get it to react. There are always Spanish children. They are everywhere. Not because Spaniards are so fertile, they're not. It is just that they take their kids everywhere. And those kids meet up with other kids and run through the streets and the bars and the shops looking for adventure while their parents sit and chat with friends and have a quiet drink. It is pervasive everywhere I have been in Spain. Dogs can be the same way. It's not uncommon to see someone sitting at a table with a dog curled up under the table whether inside or out.

The people-watching is great today. We see some amusing people, some stylish people, some punks, a lot of children, tourists, locals and students but mostly it is families.

Soon, lunch hour is over and the crowds on this corner have dried up. We walk around the town for a bit and then find a nice nook with people eating, having an ice cream or just sitting and talking. We take up a chair outside a little coffee shop and I get some coffee to keep me going.

Across the plaza is a family having lunch. They have a wide-eyed and innocent little blond boy who is fascinated by his new red ball. He will throw it, scream, and then gleefully run after it. And by run, I mean totter drunkenly on his two fat little baby legs, lean forward and then run to catch up with himself, moments away from disaster and a tumble every second. The ball rolls over to us a couple of times but like a nervous squirrel he won't come over and take it out of my hand, standing a good ten feet away and nervously smiling at me. I throw the ball back to him every time but he never warms up to us and stays very close to his parents.

Now the musicians come in. Luckily, there aren't many of them. Wandering minstrels will play a song at your table whether you want them to or not and then ask to be paid for the experience. Madrid is rife with them. In Baiona, we only see two. One of them is a drunken old man in shabby clothes playing a guitar and badly singing Elvis songs. He goes right up to the nervous little boy and starts bellowing "You ain't nothin' but a hound dog" and the boy's eyes go wide. A pile of dirt with a strange and noisy instrument seems to be trying to communicate with him! He screams and runs to his parents.

After the man leaves the child is still wide eyed. He sits near his parents with a look of shock on his face and clutches his ball tightly to his chest for a half an hour before he starts to play again.

Eventually, they move along and we decide it's our time as well. Still on the Madrid food schedule, it's four-thirty in the afternoon and we need some lunch. We make our way back to the restaurant with the tower of seafood and the terrace and the hostess greets Wendy warmly. Of course anyone who has met Wendy for longer than a minute greets her warmly. I notice that this place must be good. The tower of seafood is seriously diminished.

After looking over the menu we can't decide. Wendy thinks we should get a *parillada* of seafood, which is really, just a large selection on one plate. But they have two different varieties one of which is double the price of the other.

Our waiter is very nice, but a bit odd. For one thing, he speaks a mix of Portuguese, Spanish and English and none of them well. He can tell that Wendy is fluent in Spanish and he knows I understand English. When Wendy asks him for a detailed list of each *parillada* he tries to explain in both, but his Portuguese keeps getting mixed up in his Spanish and doesn't know the right words for all the seafood in English, so neither Wendy nor I are sure what he is trying to describe. Finally he just takes me in the restaurant and tries to point out the different varieties of seafood that come with the more expensive plate, but they are in bins and I'm still confused after his explanation. Wendy makes the executive decision to just order the more expensive of the two. The other thing that is odd is he has a hip problem and walks with a much exaggerated limp, almost throwing one leg in front of the other. Not that this takes anything away from the fact that he is exceedingly nice and very good at his job, it just seems different to have a waiter with a hip problem. Those two things don't seem to go well together.

Our food arrives and it is stunning.

We have a crab completely prepared like the one we had in Santiago. The edible guts in the thorax, chilled, the claws all broken and waiting. We have a stack of grilled tiger shrimp, a pile of cigala, two dozen *percebes*, mussels, clams, *berberechos*, *necoras* (small crabs) and more.

We keep filling up our plates with shells and the waiter keeps taking away the bodies of all those we have consumed bringing us fresh plates. Pieces of shell litter the table, and our shirts are getting splashed with olive oil and water when we snap things open. We go to town on the crab. Wendy discovers the wonders of grilled tiger shrimp and I start to leave those for her. We split the *percebes* and then I start to go to town on the cigala. This is easily one of my favorite meats, rivaling North Atlantic lobster dipped in butter, but it is so expensive we rarely have it. We have a nice stack of them and despite already feeling full; I resolve not to leave even one on the plate.

Cigala is odd to me. It's more expensive than lobster and about the size of a very large crayfish. And like a crayfish, the only thing you can eat out of it is the tail. I get a snatch of its taste when we order paella since one will come resting on the rice. I had another taste when we bought a kilo of them, cooked them up and then were still so hungry we cooked a pizza. Today, for the first time, I have all that I can handle and I'm not letting even one go to waste. Wendy decides the same thing on her percebes which I find that I am not that fond of, but is one of her favorite foods.

Finally, the seafood holocaust is over. The tiger shrimp is gone, the cigala is gone, the *percebes* are gone and most of the mussels and clams are gone. The only thing remaining is the garnishing seafood. Like the tiny crabs whose claws are smaller than the tip of my finger. I don't know why they bother to kill those things. Are you supposed to pop the whole thing in your mouth like a mint and crunch down? No idea.

It was one of, if not the, best meal of my life.

On the morning of the last day there, I discover there are flesh-eating sea gulls in the area. Wendy is at the buffet and I have just returned with a plate of food to the table we have on the terrace. Realizing I have forgotten something I turn to head back to the buffet. When I am not even two feet from our table, a seagull lands next to my plate, I rush him but he is too fast. He snags a piece of my bacon and flies off.

Who knew sea gulls ate pig.

The surrounding tables laugh and are as astonished as I am.

"So fast!" one table whispers.

For the rest of the meal, we are guarded by a knife wielding six-year-old girl who is terrified of the sea gulls and keeps chasing them off.

The Joys of Flying

Wendy and I fly home to Vermont for a "vacation." The Madrid businesses that Wendy targets close for the entire month of August. Except for a number of bars, hotels and restaurants, almost everything in Madrid closes in August. The residents all pack up and move to the mountains or the coast to escape the brutal summer heat.

Our first summer at home in Vermont is nothing like what I expect. I expect to come back to my house and have our routine be somewhat similar to Madrid. Instead we are faced with endlessly large and small details, appointments and commitments. Months of mail to go through, an annual college reunion of close friends, splitting time between my house and Wendy's dad's house on the lake, dinner with parents, friends, lunch with old work buddies, work that needs to be done on the house, dog vet appointments, car repairs, tax information that needs to be corrected, a wedding in Rhode Island. Every day brings new appointments, new things that need to be taken care of, other people that want to see us.

Wendy and I spend the last frantic day of our "vacation" packing for our flight and mailing things back to Madrid. "Things shipped back to Madrid" would be items that you can't find easily there. Things like my preferred brand of Axe deodorant ("mmm you smell nice" is very important to me and helps lead the way to something else that's even more important to me), specific toothpaste, horseradish (no, they don't have horseradish in Madrid), the instant oatmeal and pudding we like, etc. Packing can be rough when you have two homes in completely different cultures and another vacation coming up.

Here's a travel tip for you.

Never buy a gigantic suitcase.

In Florida, knowing that we would be, at times, going home for six weeks at a time, we bought two Samsonite "Megalosaur Giganticus" suitcases. We can pack our entire wardrobe, gifts, computers, books, espresso maker, porn and toys all in one bag! Won't that be the best?

Well, we were correct. We could pack everything, and the espresso maker into them. Now imagine how much they weigh and think about the fact that we live on the fifth floor. Now imagine a forty-one-year-old metrosexual with his shirt off, sweating like a fat man running a marathon as he carries a Megalosaur Giganticus suitcase down five flights of narrow spiral steps in ninety-eight degree Madrid summer heat.

"Don't fall. Don't fall. Don't fall." I keep muttering to myself as the bag sways back and forth against my chest. (Yes, against my chest. You try and lift one of those things with one hand and carry it down a hundred plus steps.)

And now imagine going back up those steps, picking up Wendy's bag and finding it a good twenty pounds heavier.

"Don't die. Don't die. Don't die."

Images of me tripping and hurling Wendy's suitcase away from me in panic as I try to stop my fall fill my brain. Images of seventy-five pounds of clothes, make up, electronics, books and gifts spewed violently down five flights of steps haunt my imagination. By the last flight of stairs I'm muttering a completely different mantra.

"Don't have a heart attack. Don't have a heart attack. Don't die. Almost there."

Of course, getting these two huge bags to fit into a standard size taxi trunk presents another challenge. Two large suitcases will fit in the trunk of a cab. Two enormous ones will not. Next time they come to pick us up I bet they bring a van.

And to top off this adventure in luggage hell, imagine us getting to the airport and having them tell us the bags are too heavy to go on the plane.

Are we having fun yet?

Back to the present. Well, we're smarter this time. The six week Vermont summer visit is over and now we're packing shit up again. And this time, we know the weight limit for the airplane. For most airlines it is two bags per person each not weighing more than fifty pounds. One bag can't weigh more than fifty pounds unless you want to pay extra then you can go up to seventy pounds in two bags.

Can you see how having one huge bag isn't that great?

Packing today takes longer than it did in Madrid because we have to weigh the bags and juggle stuff so that they make the limit without additional fees. And we're bringing back duffel bags that will contain the majority of the clothes and books we're bringing to Provence. This will save on packing time later. Yes, we are heading back to Provence.

We finish the packing and I carry the last box over to the mail and Wendy does all the paperwork to get it shipped. When we return home, her father is sitting on the steps waiting to drive us to the airport.

We get checked in with no hassles. We go get a drink in the airport bar and compare feelings about leaving Vermont to heading back to Madrid and how we hope the flights are smooth. The schedule we have planned for the next 24 hours could range in the neighborhood of "slightly hard" to "mental breakdown insane" depending on how much security, airplanes, baggage handlers and delays decide to screw with us. Usually with air travel, that is a lot.

We leave from Burlington, which is a small airport, headed to Newark, Small airport security is almost always easy. We get through with no hassles and in very little time. We read a bit in the waiting area. Wonder of wonders, we also depart on time. The flight is smooth and easy and arrives on time as well. In Newark we don't have to go through security again, don't have to pick up our luggage, and get no hassle from anyone. We have an hour and a half for dinner and find a couple seats at the bar of our favorite steak house, Gallagher's.

Two seats away from us, a man is eating smoked salmon. Next to him a man has just received an appetizer that looks delicious. A thin, young, crisp professional kid named Eddie gives us some menus and I ask him what the dish is three seats over. This is something I have learned from one of my new heroes, Anthony Bourdain, author of *Kitchen Confidential* and host of The Travel Channel's "No Reservations." In his exotic travels, not able to speak the language, he will sit down next to someone who appears to be eating something appetizing. When the waiter comes over he'll point and motion until he gets across the idea "I'll have what she's having." While the language isn't a problem, the idea remains the same.

We order a bottle of Rosemont Shiraz, the crab lump cocktail, a plate of fries and "what he's having."

"What he's having" is not on the Gallagher's menu that is posted online, but could best be described as a filet mignon *tostada*. It is essentially, small pieces of toast with bleu cheese, rare filet mignon and caramelized onions on top.

"Seriously, you could add caramelized onions to cake and it would make it taste better." – Colette Ballou

The steak is sublime. The crab is fresh and delicious. The wine, as Rosemont always is, is smooth and enjoyable. Wendy and I have a couple glasses of wine and glow at each other. Our waiter behind the bar, Eddie, is struggling to keep up with the mounting checks while simultaneously trying to flirt with an oddly attractive girl that has come in and is seated next to us. I say "oddly attractive" because the girl looks a bit hard. She has a cute face, a thin frame but nothing like a classic beauty.

When I can get his attention, I order more tostada. I pour Wendy more wine and then set my hand on her thigh and we gossip about Eddie and the oddly attractive girl. Flirting? Couple? Friends? Soon the girl leaves and Eddie turns back to us. "Where are you folks heading?"

We make small talk for fifteen minutes and then head for our flight. Great kid. We leave him a nice tip.

The stars have aligned this day. We have had a wonderful meal with a nice waiter and the flight to Madrid is also on time. Boarding is simple and there is no long wait for take-off. No queue like we've had before, waiting forty-five minutes for our place in line on the runway to come up so the plane can be on its way. We read for an hour and Wendy finds out what the in-flight movies are going to be. Kid and dog movies. I like dogs. I like dogs a lot. Too bad dog movies suck. I'm forty-two so I'm not that big a fan of kid's movies either.

We eventually drift off for three hours and then wake up. I wake up to see a little fuzzy white dog genius saving kids from a fire while simultaneously catching the arsonist and getting a bottle for a hungry baby. God damn I hate dog movies.

I try to get back to sleep and I fail. It's four a.m. our time why the hell are we both awake? Resigned to our fate we pull out our books and start to read more, all while trying to avoid looking at the screen as Rover solves the national debt and brings peace to the Middle East.

We get to Madrid three sleepy hours later and land without crashing. I always consider this a good sign. If we can get our luggage without bother, half this trip will have been hassle free. Well, except for that dog movie; that was painful.

We get into the terminal and find the screen that tells us what carousel our luggage is going to be coming out on. Around this carousel there are already a hundred people from the flight that came in before us. There are a hundred bags on the carousel and no one is touching anything. I look around for familiar passengers and see plenty, so I know this is the right place. Another flight arrives and more people come streaming in and stand at our carousel, upping the number to another hundred or more. It is now midnight at Times Square on New Year's Eve packed around the baggage oval. People press and the crowd, now seven deep, peers over shoulders for a glimpse at the hundreds of bags jamming the long conveyor belt.

No one is picking up bags.

None of these bags belong to any of the people here.

Since ten minutes have gone by, I assume there's been some kind of mix up and relinquish my spot to the hordes of people crowding me. About fifty percent of the time in the past two months of our travels when there is a delay, it is due to the baggage jerk offs in the back not caring or not knowing what the fuck they are doing. Wendy's on the job. Wendy is always on the job. She starts questioning guys in jumpsuits and badges.

"Everything is fine; your bags will be out soon." Oblivious to the fact that two hundred plus people are watching a potpourri of bags rotate in an endless circle and no is picking up anything.

"Don't know. Screen says number two."

"Not my job." Continues eating his sandwich and looks at her blankly until she goes away.

"Check with Continental," one clerk shrugs.

Wendy goes to the Continental desk and asks if they know anything. She is informed by a very nice woman that they didn't know there was a problem and would look into it right away. She comes back five minutes later shaking her head. The guys handling the luggage had it all on carts and didn't know which carousel to put it on so they just waited, not calling anyone, not guessing, just doing… nothing. The nice Continental woman tells them to put it on three. Ten minutes later we have our luggage and are speeding towards Madrid with an English-speaking taxi driver. He used to work in New York for a travel company but when 9/11 happened, the travel company lost a lot of business and had to let him go. Now he's back to Madrid with his wife and they do this and tours on the side. Nice guy.

We unload and I once again face the daunting task of carrying a lot of heavy things up a lot of stairs. No, I don't let my beautiful Spanish girl carry fifty pound bags up five flights of stairs. Commandment number one: Carry heavy things. We have five hours to get everything upstairs, unpack some of it, pack a bag for Provence, and get back to the airport thirty minutes away. Thanks to our careful planning in Vermont, oh so many hours ago, the bags for Provence are mostly packed already. A bit of switching of toiletries and electronics and we're ready to go. Sadly, the baggage jerks have screwed with us again.

Three of our bags have been searched and a portable DVD player given to Wendy by her father has been stolen. The box and its packing materials are loose in the luggage and no sign of the player. We feel violated and extremely pissed. After unpacking far more than we had planned, looking to see what else they might have broken or stolen, we finally get to lie on the bed and catch some winks. An hour later the alarm goes off and we're out the door again.

May you live in interesting times.

Indeed.

Provence and the Shower from Hell

Tonight we're flying Ryanair. I can't imagine a lower cost airline to fly. Our round trip flight for both of us is costing less than a hundred and fifty Euros (two-hundred dollars.) But you have to know what you're doing to get that fare. Bags are limited to fifteen kilograms (thirty-five lbs.), so pack light and pack everything in duffel bags. There's no free food, no assigned seating, no in-flight movie. The seats don't even recline.

Seeing as how we are Ryanair experts we plan ahead. We pay an extra three Euros and get priority boarding for the flight there and back. As we watch people struggle to make weight or shell out extra cash for their hard, over-weight suitcases, and stand in a line that will be ignored by half of the Europeans sitting down, Wendy and I are breezing through check-in with bags under-weight, board the plane first and with food.

Feeling mighty smart. Yup. Mighty smart indeed.

We look out the window and point and laugh at the gigantic bags being loaded under our plane and wonder how much those people had to pay for their budget fare that was suddenly not so budget.

Once in the air Ryanair starts selling lottery tickets (not kidding), perfumes, stuffed dolls, knives (totally kidding), minor electronics and other sundry merchandise. It's like a JC Penney catalog in the sky. Since the seats don't recline, I can't get to sleep. I buy a coffee and read some more of Anthony Bourdain's *A Cooks Tour*.

It's a short, uneventful flight. About ninety minutes into it I start to get jittery and keep looking at the stewardesses. They appear calm. That feeling like we're falling out of the sky must just be our descent. Wendy sees my nervousness and gently takes hold of my hand and assures me that's all it is. It is just the descent. I am still not a huge fan of flying.

Landing and luggage is smooth as silk. I am so counting my blessings for this day. Some minor hiccups but so far – I am still not insane or breaking down in any way. All we have to do is pick up our rental car, drive an hour to Brignoles (pronounced BREEG-NO-LEES... okay I'm totally lying it's pronounced BRIN-Yo) and find our way to the summer chateau (pronounced lying-by-the-pool-reading-and-drinking-fine-wine-in-the-French-countryside.)

The rental car is waiting for us and since we have great printed directions this time, we opt out of the Garmin "Neverlost."

Within ten minutes we're lost.

Luckily, Wendy gets Colette on the phone, describes a few landmarks and signs and she knows right where we are - going in the wrong direction.

Not quite so luckily, when we go to turn around I discover the car has no reverse.

We get off the freeway to turn around. I head down a road I think will put us going in the opposite direction but quickly find out I'm wrong. I pull into what looks like a wagon trail and attempt to back out onto the road. Only... the car won't go into reverse. I look at the diagram on top of the stick shift: yup, all the way to the right and down. Again. Nothing. Again. A whir of gears signifying nothing. Again. Damn it!

I'm going to have to push the car out of where we are and Wendy doesn't drive a stick. I tell her to yank on the emergency brake when I push it far enough back onto the road. I get out and throw my back into it. Since the car weighs about two hundred pounds this works just fine and Wendy cranks on the emergency brake when I've pushed us back five feet. I climb back in and maneuver us back onto the freeway.

Wendy and I debate about if we should return to the car dealership and get a different car. I finally decide yes.

Colette calls us back wondering how we're doing. We explain. She informs us that reverse is all the way to the right and down. At the same moment that she is whispering this in Wendy's ear, a long dormant memory stirs to life.

I look closely at the stick shift. There is a ring in the middle of the stick shift.

I lift the ring up, move the stick all the way to the right and down and the car slides smoothly into reverse.

At fifty miles an hour.

Yeah.

I'm completely lying to you again. What is with me today? (I actually pulled over and tested this and then we continued on.)

From there, it is a relatively simple and painless matter of making our way to the summer house. They have some mutton in a variety of sauce, garnish, some bread and some red wine. Collette assures me it is mutton and not lamb claiming she has explained to our hosts my eating prejudices. I don't care if she's lying to me, as long as I don't know it's lamb. Joining me for dinner are our two hosts Carole and Pierre Yves (Mathieu's parents), Vero, (the model whose wedding we attended earlier this year), a CFO of a private aviation company, two spies and a former girlfriend who now owns her own PR firm in Paris. I try not to snort when I laugh, wipe food on my sleeve, spill wine or in any other way embarrass myself among these amazing people. I consider asking for some ketchup for my mutton but refrain.

It's been a long, long day.

Despite that, Wendy and I can't sleep and we read for another couple hours after dinner. We awaken eleven hours later, dreadfully late for breakfast and slightly late for lunch.

I badly need to wash the collective dust, grime, airplane smell, pressed humanity and my own sweat and stink off of me before lunch. Something else I discover different about Europe is the bathrooms. In the guest house there are two bathrooms and one toilet. Each bathroom contains a shower, towels, shelves, a mirror and a sink. The toilet contains just that- a closet sized room with a toilet in it. This room is so small that when sitting down you have to turn your knees to the right and scrunch your ass cheeks up to close the door.

Wendy has used the shower and is getting dressed when I have my first of many encounters with the shower from hell. Common to all places I have been in Europe, the water comes out of a spray hose attached to a faucet four feet below. There is a mount about a foot above my head to put the shower head into, but when placed in its receptacle all it sprays is the wall it's mounted on. So, I quickly learn the most effective (and only) method is 1) you soak yourself down with the hose, 2) put it in its holder above your head, the water spraying against the wall while you soap up 3) you bring it down, point it at your body, 4) find out all the hot water has run out, and 5) scream.

"Jame?" Wendy hollers into my bathroom.

"Yeah?"

"Lunch is ready, they're waiting on us."

Screaming - "I'll be right there!"

When I make it to the table, shivering and barely dry, everyone else has already arrived and is patiently sitting, hands folded and lightly conversing. Lunch is a French macaroni salad with mozzarella balls, red peppers, tomatoes, black olives and instead of heavy mayonnaise, a light vinaigrette sauce. The CFO of the private aviation company is gone; the model, PR firm owner, the spies, the struggling writer and parents remain. There is conversation, but I'm not awake yet despite my sub-zero dip into a blast of ice water.

After lunch, I'm wondering who do I have to kill to get some caffeine? Wendy emerges from the house and asks me "Do you want coffee?"

"Yes, God, yes. After a thirty-five hour day and then eleven hours of sleep, I am dying."

Everyone has coffee after lunch. A big steaming blissful tray of tea cups filled with coffee is served and ten minutes later I'm starting to feel human again.

I help clean up as best as I can and then return to my book at the table. My hosts go down to the pool while Colette, Wendy and Mathieu are all working on their computers. I read for a bit more and then, believing that I should show my appreciation for the pool and the view we have been invited to enjoy for a week, I join Pierre Yves and Carole down by the pool. As soon as I get down there, another thought enters my mind. What if they came down here for some quiet time away from their endless stream of guests? They are probably wondering when they can get away from this filthy American. They can't escape me. Ah, the joys of being socially inept.

I bake in the sun for a bit and then, determined to get some exercise this week, I decide to do some laps in the pool. Apparently, running isn't the same as swimming. I'm able to do a measly five laps before I have to rest. I read a bit more then struggle through five more.

Wrapped in a red towel I come back up to the terrace after reading for a bit and ask Colette if it's okay to sit on the chairs which have white outdoor cushions on them and she assures me it's fine. Thirty minutes later my female host, Carole, is asking me to stand up.

The white cushion is now a milky pink.

My wet towel has stained the cushion.

Sigh.

Mathieu, Wendy and I are heading into town in fifteen minutes, so I ask Mathieu where the bathroom is in the main house. He points in the vague direction of two doors. The first one has a sink, a shower and a bidet? A foot washer? Is it a urinal with faucets?

"Mathieu, before I embarrass myself…"

"Other door."

Thank God.

Staining a cushion and then peeing in the foot washer probably wouldn't endear me too much to our hosts.

We go into town to get grocery supplies and champagne for dinner, passing multiple vineyards on the short ride. Brignole is much like the rest of the French countryside I've seen - lush and green. There are beautiful yet steeply jagged, treacherous looking mountains off in the distance, nothing like the slow rolling Green Mountains of my home state of Vermont where you could walk to the top of one in an afternoon. The country roads are barely big enough for two Smart cars to pass, and there are roundabouts every mile or so. The town of Brignole is like a postcard; quaint and uncluttered, full of little shops, a grocery store, a rotisserie chicken place and pizza trucks.

We stop at a beautiful wine store that is all things wine and wine openers. Lovingly displayed are shelves after shelves of red, white, rose, and champagne. In the back of the store, slightly out of context, there are two, six foot tall, four-foot wide, clear barrels with gas hoses coming out of them. Like a filling station, you can come in with your own gallon jugs, boxes or barrels and just fill them with red or white table wine from a gas hose.

Beautiful girl on my arm? Check. Well rested? Check. Caffeinated? Check. Full without being stuffed from lunch? Check. Relaxed from lying by the pool reading? Check. 400 gallons of wine attached to a gas hose five feet away. Check.

I'm pretty sure I'm in heaven.

Wendy and I would like to buy the wine tonight as a thank you to our hosts. Mathieu points out a couple bottles that I deem "not expensive enough" so he points us to a twenty six Euro bottle of wine and informs us that it is Carole's favorite. It looks like we have a winner. We pick up a couple other items and head back to the house.

As I type this, the mistral is blowing hard and fierce. As described by Peter Mayle in *A Year in Provence* it is enough to drive you mad. It has been blowing since morning and it is now after four in the afternoon. The trees shake, the house rattles, table umbrellas are blown over, doors and windows bang open and shut, my hair keeps flying about my face (particularly into my eyes) and the French sit quietly reading in the gale unaware that anything is amiss as their newly bought pool chairs blow down the hill. I write for a while on the porch but then, maddened by the wind, I decide to go sit by the pool and read for a bit because it looks a bit more sheltered and out of the blustery weather. Wendy and Colette are already down there, discussing all things important to women.

The book I'm trying to read is maddeningly boring, the wind is still strong down here, and I really should be writing. After a half an hour of reading, I resign myself to my fate and head inside to get some work done before dinner.

So far, I've felt a bit of an outcast. While our hosts are genial and kind, I'm the only one here that doesn't speak a lick of French. Wendy is fluent in English, Spanish and Italian, speaks some French and knows a bit of Russian. Carole, Pierre and Vero can understand English if I speak slowly enough but even then sometimes they need a translation from Mathieu. I've tried my best to help with the meals when I can, stay out of the way when I can't, and make myself as unobtrusive as possible. My star achievement so far was showing Mathieu how to turn the *jamon* we gave him so long ago to a different position where I believe there is a better cut of meat. Luckily, I was right, and he gets a great deal from that area of the bone. I am very proud.

It is now dinner time. As mentioned earlier in the day, we have bought some champagne, Carole's favorite. We all gather on the porch overlooking the mountains for appetizers and Champagne. Presented to us are seven empty glasses, a plate of *jamon* and black and green olive tapenades. Mathieu then goes into the kitchen and gets the first bottle of champagne and Carole cries out with glee when she sees it. Mathieu explains that it, as well as the *jamon* is from us. Carole thanks us, hugs and kisses to both of us and then calls up a friend. Colette explains that she is calling to gloat. Translating that Carole is telling her friend how good her family is and how well they take care of her, that once again she is drinking champagne and having *jamon* on her back porch overlooking the mountains before dinner.

The *jamon* is fantastic. The black olive tapenades on little pieces of toast are much better than the green tapenade and it is easy to see why this champagne is Carole's favorite. When we surprise her with another bottle, she again gives a little gleeful cry, hands become outstretched offering hugs, kisses all around again.

And now I'm "in like Flynn." Did you know that expression actually refers to Errol Flynn and his capacity to seduce women? Maybe it's the Champagne, but suddenly I'm feeling a lot more comfortable, almost like I belong here and am no longer an intruding American, tolerated for the sake of Mathieu and Colette. Nothing Pierre Yves or Carole has done has given me that impression; it's just my neuroses talking.

As we sit, sip and talk Pierre spies an eagle and points it out to Wendy. *"Regard! Voir le cet ouest de vol d'aigle ? Il est très rare et spécial. Il mange seulement des lézards et des serpents."*

Wendy tells me he was pointing out a rare hawk that eats only snakes and lizards. I'm so tired of being the only mono-lingual person anywhere I go. Everywhere in Europe people speak two, three sometimes even four languages. Pierre points again and tells Wendy that the hawk lives on that mountain over there.

"And how do you know that? Did you track the hawk over there?"

Pierre looks confused for a moment then laughs. "No, no, nothing like that. It says so in my guidebook."

Too many good stories and champagne start to affect my memory. I should do something to make sure I remember all this. I go down to the guest house and get my voice recorder. I have so many notes to add. They see me recording and ask what I'm doing. I explain about my writing, *Neither Here Nor There*, *A Year in Provence*, *A Parrot in a Pepper Tree* and other travel memoirs. I'm writing about my exploration of Europe titled *I'm Not an Alcoholic I'm Just European*. Collette translates and they all laugh.

Dinner is couscous - something I have never had before. There is also *merguez* sausage, beef and mutton. And more wine. Always more wine. Over dinner I am asked my impressions of Europe.

I explain to them my love of the liberal attitudes of the places I have visited. America feels so conservative now, almost oppressive.

Nudity is something many fear or are ashamed of in America, even in art, but all over Europe I have seen statues with zero modesty, breasts and penises exposed, frescoes on bar walls of nude women in bed together, paintings in public places that would be illegal and cause an uproar in America. I explain with shame Attorney General John Ashcroft covering up the statue of *Lady Justice's* bare breast with a sheet. I explain that there seems to be less fear of everything in general here. Life just…is.

The typical European isn't exposed to countless warnings of hurricanes, exploding lighters, supposedly toxic chemicals that might or might not be in your home or food and affecting your children. Won't someone please think of the children! Everything here moves at a slower pace and is filled with so much less worry.

I then move on to the history and sense of age to buildings and statues in Europe; the amazing, mythological beauty of Paris and Madrid, the individuality of the countries; the individuality even within different regions of the countries, with different food, customs and even variations of languages. Spain has four languages within its borders. Four! I explain how all of that so lacks in America. You can get a hamburger, a pizza, Chinese and Mexican food at any town from coast to coast in America and everyone will understand you for thousands of square miles. And that's a good thing, but the diversity of having limited choices, limited speech, and until recently, different currency, in different towns in Europe is eye opening.

I pause for breath and they buttress my point by explaining Napoleon had trouble commanding his army and had to build his units carefully. People from the north of France didn't speak the same language as those from the south. The difference between each of the countries is so vast and everything in America is so homogenized. You can drive 700 kilometers in America and you might not have even left the state yet. You travel 700 kilometers in Europe you're speaking a different language, the food is completely different and your money is now worthless pieces of colored paper.

Pierre Yves speaks up and tells us, "Charles De Gaulle once said 'It is impossible to rule a country that has 350 different kinds of cheese'" which illicit laughter from all of us.

Carole speaks up and points out how they smelled smoke in the Empire State Building and a policeman took control and said "Okay, everyone line up, we have to leave," and she was amazed they did just that. Everyone filed up and left in an orderly line except the French and the other Europeans who had no idea what to do.

Wendy brings up Ryanair and how we have learned you just don't stand in line when you're in Europe.

Then comes the discussion on the drinking of alcohol. There is this stigma attached to drinking in the States. If you have a drink a day you are considered an alcoholic. Here, it's just a pastime. It's a part of the daily social hour.

In some cases it's a part of competition. Pierre explains about the "Marathon du Medoc" he participates in. One of the many marathons he participates in actually. This one is special. The course winds its way through the French countryside, visiting vineyard after vineyard for a sampling of their wares. Yes, the usual twenty-six miles of this. Two thoughts glare brightly in my mind at this image.

1) You would never find this in the states.

2) I have a new goal.

That night Wendy, Vero, Mathieu and I play speed Monopoly. Three quarters of the properties are handed out to the players. Anything not passed out can be bought for its regular price. Wendy is handed Boardwalk and Park Place. Only, this is the French version so it's the Louvre and the Eiffel Tower.

I discover Monopoly is a lot like the game of Magic.

It becomes clear only a short time into the game that either Mathieu or Wendy is going to be the winner. They have twelve properties between them; many of them with houses. I have a tiny six properties and Vero has the railroads. Vero decides not much later that she is going to back Mathieu and sells him all four of her railroads for six million francs. A pittance of what they are worth and a small percent of what he has in cash. Seeing this, I know the next logical step is to throw in with Wendy. When I pass "Go" and get two million francs, I un-mortgage all my property and then sell everything I own to Wendy for 10 thousand francs.

Now it's a battle of the titans.

Well, you would think so wouldn't you?

Vero decides to circle the board, never landing on anything Mathieu or Wendy owns, but multiple times, landing on "Chance", "Go to Jail" and "Free Parking" so that her fortune soon exceeds eighteen million francs. Mathieu decides to go to jail a number of times, land on his own properties and despite repeated trips around the board, never lands on a Wendy property. I on the other hand, promptly land on a Mathieu property and he gets all my money. Fifteen minutes later, Wendy has sold all her houses and mortgaged everything she has. Vero now has a fortune of thirty million francs, having never had to pay rent to anyone, and buys Wendy out so we can go to bed.

While we had a good time, it reminded me so very much of Magic. Sure there's skill in the game. But sometimes, the luck factor is just overwhelming.

That night while reading, we are besieged by hornets the size of my little finger. Your *whole* little finger. Look at your little finger. Yes, that big. They are drawn to the light and keep flying in the open windows. When they eventually settle down, close to the light, I whack them with my book or a shoe. Five die before we turn the lights off. Five gigantic wasps. Mathieu tells me they are very dangerous, four or five stings can kill you. I believe him. Looking them up on the internet the next day, I find they are not a native species but an invader called the Asian hornet, *Vespa velutina*. These vile things are destroying the honeybee population of France by feeding honeybee larvae to their young.

Man, and I thought eating lamb was bad. These hornets feed babies to their babies!

Awful.

I'm not quite sure why they are a problem to get rid of. The only thing that was attracted to the light at night was those hornets. Set up a good old American bug zapper and watch the carnage.

At around six a.m., a good sized storm rolls in. Outside I hear thunder and lighting and... flip flops? When I peek my head out the door I see Mathieu collecting towels from outside and shutting windows. I ask if I can help with anything and he tells me that no, he is done. I go back to bed and wonder if I'll be able to get back to sleep.

I am. I dream that I am driving on a rutted and pitted road. There is road construction in progress and I am trying to avoid the flag-women and machinery, but it's always tricky and I am very nervous. I get too close to a steamroller and it backs into my RAV4, crushing the entire front of it like bad tinfoil. I know that my Honda Element is behind me filled with friends. I climb into the driver's seat and take that over. A few minutes later a grater has scrapped against the side, keying the entire right side of the vehicle in a foot and half long line of scratched paint and dented metal, almost wrecking the entire car. Still we continue, the wheel rubbing against the wheel well, the smell of burning rubber thick in the air. Finally, the road is so bad we cannot continue. We get out and head back the way we have come and it is even worse than the road we just drove, transforming in the way that dreams have the power to do. I climb over an embankment; there is a car at the top with its trunk open and the trunk is filled with water. Teetering on the top of the embankment, I look inside and see half a dozen snakes in the trunk of the car and I know they are going to strike at me. And I'm right. Soon, I have two in my arm and one on my face. I punch them as hard as I can, but as always in my dreams, the blows are like pillows. It is then that I know I am dreaming. I continue to strike at the snakes, willing myself, knowing it's a dream, to smash them in the face with terrific force, but nothing happens. The blows still land as soft as a caress.

From a long way away Wendy says "Yes, it's gorgeous."

Colette answers her with "Yes, I think it's really nice."

I awaken. Wendy comes back into the room and lies down next to me. "What part of Colette was gorgeous?"

She smacks me. "We were talking about the day. The storm has passed and it looks beautiful out there."

"What time is it?"

"It's eleven-thirty."

I guess I'm still a bit jetlagged. But, I grudgingly, groggily, painfully roll my way out of bed and find some shorts and head for the bathroom. Since Wendy has showered long ago, there should be hot water. I'm right. Oh God is there hot water! I turn on the hot water all the way and notice there is a great deal of pressure. None of that wispy water conservation here. I'm going to have a shower like I used to in college where the pressure is great enough to blast you out the door and flay the skin from your bones. Now I start to add cold water and the shower becomes like a fire hose. I can barely control it with one hand. I stick my hand into the water and scream. Despite the addition of the cold water, it is still as molten and flesh searing as McDonald's coffee. I add more cold water, the hose becoming a powerful snake trying to escape my grasp. I tentatively stick my hand into the water. Yow! Still hot, but tolerable. I step into the shower and start blasting the top layer of skin off myself like I haven't been able to do in over two decades.   Ah, this is heaven; a scorching skin blasting torrent of water coursing over my body. Less than a minute later, the water starts to go cold.

"No! No!" I scream, bewildered. How can this be, the water was so hot!?

And then it's gone and I am holding a cold mountain stream in my right hand feeling betrayed and confused. And cold. Let us not forget the cold. Again, I am forced to have a cold shower, shivering as I wash my hair and curse this horrible, horrible thing. I go up to the main house and make myself a bowl of coffee. Speaking of which, let's review a few of the things I have learned in my time in France:

Morning coffee is drunk out of bowls you lift to your mouth. Usually a large amount of milk is poured into a small amount of coffee and sipped like a child with a bowl of soup.

You close the bathroom door when you leave, which means you're always knocking or tentatively pulling on the handle to see if anyone is inside.

Water comes with or without gas. There are two varieties served at every meal, one carbonated, one not.

The cheese course is after dinner, usually four to six choice cheeses that are usually spread on bread. I chose to be decadent and have butter and cheese on my bread.

Lunch is at 1:30, unless you are a jetlagged American and have missed breakfast.

Preceding the evening meal is wine and appetizers at 8:00 and dinner is served whenever the appetizers are done.

Wine comes in boxes or bottles or gallon jugs if you prefer to pour your own. Usually bought from the local vineyard of choice, of which there are many.

We have a meal of Caesar salads in the early afternoon, then I retire to the pool to read a successful travel writer and think, "I can write better than this" and digest. An hour later Wendy and I decide to go for a run. We walk down the hill and walk along the access road which is half a kilometer long to warm up. On the way down we see electric fencing on one property and wonder what they are trying to keep inside. It's only about two feet high and spaced about eight inches apart. It couldn't keep rabbits, birds, horses or anything small enough to fit through the cracks through, what could they be raising? We decide it must be goats or sheep.

Walking along the access road we pass in front of one property that has three medium size hounds. Two of them bark and wag their tails at us, excited by the prospect of something happening in front of them. The third is also excited. Excited like a serial killer watching a hooker walking alone on a deserted stretch of back country road. His tail is not wagging and he is not happy to see movement. He wants blood. He wants to get out from behind the three-foot fence and attack us.

"That one dog is not joking" I tell Wendy.

"What? What do you mean?"

"See how the other dogs bark and wag their tails? See how that one doesn't wag his tail instead his barks are intermingled with growls and has a murderous, hateful gleam in his eyes? Yeah, he wants to get at us, but not to not play like the others."

"That fence isn't very high; maybe we shouldn't go this way?"

"I can handle him if he jumps over, don't worry. I can beat up one dog."

We start our run and when we pass by the property again, the dogs are inside. We are a bit relieved their master has brought them in. Behind us there is a roar. We barely get out of the way of a speeding dirt bike flying down the road. Five seconds behind him is a policeman chasing him, sirens screaming.

We reach the end of the road, turn around run back, repeat, dogs out again, this time with a master who quiets them but murderous dog still glares at us as we run by as if to say "I'll get you Dorothy. You and your little dog, too!"

Now it is so peaceful. There is something special about running by fields of vineyards and quiet country French homes. I think about the two different partners I have had and how much they have both suited me at different times in my life. The first when all I wanted was to stay home and play video games was perfect for me then. Now, perfect for this time in my life, The Beautiful Wendy who has shown me all there is to this world and made me alive again. I have been blessed.

We finish our run at the twenty-five minute mark and head back up the hill.

The shower from hell scalds me.

Wendy is at the pool, and since the time is beer-thirty, I get us a couple drinks and join her. The mistral is still blowing like mad. It makes reading nearly impossible for me. Pierre and Carole just ignore it, reading their magazines and books with little care that the pages are almost blown from their hands and flap wildly in the breeze. We relax for a bit, I do some writing then help Wendy make a pasta salad. I discover Anthony Bourdain is right; you only need one, sharp, big-ass knife not fifteen in a wooden block. I discover that tomatoes cut much better with a big-ass knife.

Appetizers and dinner are served and we again discuss my fascination with Europe and my disgust with how they outlawed vibrators in Alabama in 2004.

The mistral is *still* blowing. The wind is cutting into me and by now, the Vermont boy of the bunch, I am wearing a long sleeved shirt and jeans. Normally, I resist the cold better than anyone around me. Pierre Yves is still in his shorts and shirtless.

We have chorizo, *jamon*, black and green olives, pistachios and *pastis* (a licorice flavored liquor mixed with water) for the wine and appetizer course. Again I am lost to these people who travel so much more than I ever have. Wendy, as always, amazes me with her knowledge, talking about how each culture in Europe has a different licorice-tasting drink, giving examples of each one. Then the talk turns to Catalan, Spain and how under Franco it was illegal to speak the native language, requiring the natives to speak strictly Spanish. We talk of cultures struggling to survive in today's rapidly homogenizing world. In Catalonia, they have actually diverted government money to fund porn movies as long as the actors only speak Catalan. "Why?" Wendy asks. "Why? What good does this do their children? Who speaks Catalan anymore?"

Colette isn't able to join us for the wine and appetizer course as she is struggling with a million dollar deal that has threatened to blow up in her face for the past three days. Some vacation. What am I doing with these people? How did my hayseed self get invited to join these people?

The mistral continues to blow like a mild hurricane. Pierre and Mathieu enlighten me to a similar wind in Switzerland called the *foehn,* and how it has the same effect on the populace as the mistral. It's actually illegal to hold court when it's blowing because the wind makes everyone so angry they are afraid the judge will lose his temper and imprison someone for life for jaywalking.

Talk then turns to the Swiss and the different impressions of them. Being an American, I explain that when we think of the Swiss we think of porn movies, blonds and skiing. Carole, Mathieu and Pierre Yves mention watches, banks and neutrality. And then the highlight of the evening, Mathieu delves into touchy ground.

"Jamie, maybe you will be honest with me. I have asked this question a lot but no one will give me a clear answer for fear of offending me – "What do Americans really think of the French?"

I choke on my wine.

"Surrender monkey" was a term mentioned in a book I read a few days ago and Bill Bryson in *Neither Here Nor There* remarks "…because let's face it, the French Army couldn't beat a girl's soccer team." but I go for the more politically correct answers since I would like to eat tonight.

"When American's think of France and the French, we think of beautiful women, fine wine and the best chefs in the world."

"Yes, yes… but what else?

Wendy tactfully says "Surrender monkeys!"

I go white and hear, "What? What does that mean?"

Wendy gets up from the table to use the bathroom. I shrug and make the pouring motion with my thumb and pinky finger and roll my head back in the gesture of "I don't know, I think she's had too much wine." The conversation moves on.

"And what's up with Freedom Fries? Do you know how funny we thought that was?"

We talk about the age of America and the age of Europe. I recount us going into a Baptist church in Berlin and saw a pastor's podium that had been in use since 1623. Wendy leaned over to me and says quietly in a voice reserved for church "That podium is older than our country."

Talk moves on to how the world is fascinated with Americans. The French are fascinated with Americans. Why? Why are the French fascinated with Americans?

Carole says "Because you are like really big children."

Dinner that night was fried potatoes, roast chicken and a salad. In France, salad is lettuce and dressing; nothing else. The meal is wonderful, the conversation is fascinating and by the end of it, I have a nice happy wine glow and exclaim "This place is wonderful and I am never leaving." Our hosts look at me for a moment in abject horror and then laugh. Everyone laughs.

Wine is flowing like water. It is my job to pour, and I keep everyone's glass full and before I know it, we've gone through another bottle. Mathieu's job is to get more wine, and he is almost continually standing and going to get us another bottle. Finally, the mistral drives us all inside and we have dessert in there. We have a chocolate mousse cake and continue to talk about French versus the Americans. Mathieu compares the French to the Vulcans because "they are very logical and analytical." Carole points out that with Americans it's not uncommon to meet someone and ten minutes later they proclaim they love you and you are their best friend for life. Everything with Americans is so big and expansive and some of it feels fake to the French.

We get to bed at 1:00 a.m. and the mistral is *still* blowing.

The next day we go to the *marche*, the French market.

On the walk into the market, Wendy and Colette are regaling me with the fine purchases they have made there: "Wine, soap, towels, things to bring back to Madrid, cookery, all manner of stuff."

I take a look around.

It looks like a Bed, Bath and Beyond threw up on a flea market.

There are stalls of honey, jam and beer, used clothes, olives, snails and sausages, cheap jewelry and table after table of five Euro watches. Just out of curiosity, I ask Mathieu "Have *you* ever bought anything here?

"Pizza."

Deep in the market, a man bent from the ravages of time is handing out leaflets. Mathieu refuses to take one and he and the little man get into a polite but spirited discussion.

"What was that about?

"He is a member of the Communist party, trying to convince me his system is right. I told him if he can point to one country in the world where that system is working out well, I'd become a Communist on the spot."

I laugh.

We make our way deep into the market to order pizza to be picked up later. Pizza in Provence is a bit different than pizza in the states. It has a very thin crust, very little sauce, a light dusting of cheese and possibly an unpitted black olive or three. As with most things I'm experiencing over here, ordering is done without hurry, and with lots of conversation. We are the only people in line and it takes us fifteen minutes to place an order for five pizzas to be picked up later. Understand that this entire job entails a woman writing "five pizzas for later" on a piece of paper.

Wendy and I check out the sausage table. There are choices of donkey, pig, and wild boar sausage. Yes, you read that correctly – donkey sausage.

Wendy wants a picture of the sausage and the guy running the stall holds up his hand in a "peace" symbol behind her head just as I'm about to snap and then ducks away, too fast for me to catch. I laugh and Wendy looks at me perplexed. When I go to take another picture, he holds up a huge French flag behind her, grinning wildly and then yanks it away again as I convulse with laughter. Wendy looks around "What? What?" But the man is now standing innocently with his hands in his pockets and shrugs.

We buy four sausages and some olive tapenade from him and he compliments Wendy on her French and asks in English, "Where are you from? England?" We tell him America and he grins. "America! Welcome to France! You enjoy your time in France, okay?"

We tell him we will. As we walk away with our stuff Wendy references the current political talking points and whispers to me "It's very clear the French hate America."

We roam around a bit, Wendy and Colette buying some soap and then we return home for an afternoon of wine, pool and nap time. I fall asleep immediately.

I wake up and head to the main house for some espresso and discover we only have one package of it left. I inform Colette that we'll need to pick some up tomorrow and she tells me, "We'll have to pick them up tonight because nothing is open on Sunday. Can you go get them?"

Sure, the main town is only ten miles of back roads and two roundabouts away; what could go wrong? I have no cell phone, no idea what the phone number at this house is, no Garmin "Neverlost," no idea of even the address, I've only been to town twice (in the back seat) and I don't speak a lick of French. If I get lost, it will only be a matter of days, not hours, before I return, why not?

But, I'm not the kind of guy who says "no, I can't do that." None of the men in my family are. I descend the mountain into Brignole proper... and promptly get lost. But, luckily, I immediately know I'm lost and I've taken meticulous mental notes on what turns I've taken and retrace my steps. Once again back on fairly familiar territory, I try a new route and once again find myself in an unfamiliar part of town. Okay, let's back-track again. The third time's the charm, right? At least I can get back to this little roundabout every time (every time being a staggering "twice.") And, as luck would have it, third time is the charm and I find the wine store mentioned earlier. The grocery store next to it is packed with people that look like they are stocking up for a long winter blizzard.

"Oh my God, tomorrow is Sunday! Buy enough food to feed us if there's a nuclear holocaust and the store never opens again!"

I buy a reasonable facsimile of what I need, and when I get to the counter the tiny little French girl running it gestures wildly to me, and I have no idea what she wants. She look around, I set my things down, I pick them up, I point at myself to make sure she's talking to me, nothing helps. "Perdona, no parlez Francais." She finally stops ringing up the people in front of me, comes over, grabs me by the hand, pulls me five feet forward and shuts a gate behind me that says "Closed" in French. Ah, she is closing her register. She wanted me to come forward and pull the gate after me. As Bill Bryson says "being in a foreign country and not knowing the language is like being five years old again." To me, it feels more like being the shortest kid in the high school and getting pantsed in front of the head cheerleader every day.

I get rung up and make it to my car without incident (yay!) and drive in what I think is the way home. As I come to the second roundabout, there is a very fetching long-haired blond girl in shorts hitch-hiking on the side of the road. Options spring to mind. I could pick her up and drive her two miles up the road if she is going in the direction at the roundabout that I am. I could bring her home for dinner with the coffee. I can just imagine the startled looks (and screams) as I drive up into the mountains, unable to explain I'm inviting her to dinner. I could give her a ride. She could pull a knife on me, steal the car and leave me in a ditch. Or, I could just drive on.

168

Wisely remembering that I don't know the local language and have no idea what she would tell me about where she is going, I decide to err on the side of caution and just drive by her outstretched leg and thumb.

Around the next bend are eight police officers stopping cars. They look very casual as they talk with the three cars ahead of me. At this point I'm thinking – no passport. No cell phone. Dead hitch-hiker in the trunk; this is going to be bad. Except that dead hitch-hiker part. Man, I'm so glad I didn't pick her up.

Oddly enough, they wave the guy ahead of me through, and then wave me through. I have no idea what's going on, all I know is I'm happy. And up ahead is the road I recognize as the road up the mountain to where I'm staying tonight.

Like a mighty hunter of old, I have gone forth into the wild, slain coffee and brought it home for the morning. If there is anyone more manly than me at this very moment, I don't know who it could be.

Wendy rushes into my arms when I get back: "Oh my God you made it! How did you do that?"

She is very happy I made it back. I am very happy I made it back. Life is good.

I triumphantly return to the kitchen and show my bounty to Colette. Sadly, I notice my box of coffee is slightly different than the coffee on the counter and I ask Colette for a translation of two words on the box. Dryly she says "Danger: Poison." I look shocked for a half a second then I see she is smiling. Then, as usual, it is time for drinks and appetizers on the terrace. Is it any wonder Europeans are so relaxed?

That evening, Mathieu cuts the neck off a champagne bottle to celebrate our wonderful vacation. He moves away from the table to the edge of the terrace with a champagne bottle and a huge knife. He then holds the bottle at a forty-five degree angle at arm's length, strokes the neck several times with the knife and then with great force strokes to the end and beyond. The rim and cork of the bottle fly twenty yards towards the pool.

We all clap and settle in for appetizers and conversation, where I realize Provence has something that I do not love so much: Bees. Not only the aforementioned Asian bees that are attracted to light, but also the smaller bees that harass you at the pool while reading and are attracted to the appetizers. They keep bothering Wendy, and no matter how many I kill, more show up.

Tonight's supper is pizza for the four of us, Carole and Pierre Yves having returned home that afternoon while we were at the market. You might think that five pizzas would be too much for four people, but these are Italian style pizzas with a thin crust and only lightly covered with sauce and cheese. While delicious and pure, they are not the size and weight of American pizzas. Conversation is light and we make an early night of it.

The next morning we drive to the airport to return home. In view are some amazing mountains, the Maritime Alps. Used to the rolling green hills of Vermont, these look like something out of a fantasy novel. In Vermont, you can walk to the top of any mountain you see. They gently slope up to their full height and while it might be a long walk through brambles and scrub brush, interspersed with trees and streams, you can climb to the top of any one of them. These mountains are of a different breed entirely. Smashing through the earth like a jagged spear, not a one of them looks like it could be ascended without serious block and tackle. They look like mountains that harbor orcs and dragons.

I'm driving a car a little bigger than a matchbox at 120 kilometers an hour and people are passing me like I'm standing still. The slipstream of gigantic trucks keep dragging me off course and almost sucking me under them like a bug in a vacuum cleaner. Wendy is navigating and I'm trying to look at the mountains while simultaneously trying to keep us alive. Wendy points out "Montagne Sainte-Victoire" the most famous mountain in Provence, because the painter Paul Cézanne painted it frequently from his home nearby.

The forests are thick with the tall, thin cypresses unique to Europe. It's amazing how similar and yet completely alien this country is to my home state. With all the greenery it reminds me of home, then I'll come around a corner and see jagged troll dwelling mountains, the ocean, and row after row of vineyards. It is a shame to leave it.

Priority passes work at Ryanair again and we get to board first. Behind us, the Ryanair employee completely ignores the lines that have formed, casually drops the rope and lets everyone just run for it. Ah, Europe!

The Burning of the Bulls in Candeleda

This weekend we are going to Candeleda, for Candy Lee Laballe's wedding. That is not a joke or a typo. Candy is living the female expat-in-love-with-Spain dream. She is marrying a Spaniard; which also means marrying into a Spanish family and into a Spanish town.

This isn't always that great a thing. Many women in love with Spain think it is what they want, and then find out the difficulties of cross-cultural relationships. For one thing, Spanish men are notoriously hard to figure out in romance. Many of my female friends have told me of a date going well then a second date going well then the man ignores phone calls and messages for a month and then calls again. A third date is scheduled which also is perfect. A fourth date happens and the Spaniard starts talking about children and where they will live and how big the wedding will be. Then he vanishes off the face of the earth for a few months. One day, completely out of the blue, the phone rings. It is the man she was falling in love with and sadly, thought he must have died. And then when he calls and asks her out for dinner and on that same phone call, makes more testaments of love, she can't believe it. And then she starts to wish he had died. She stares at the phone in disbelief. Yes, it's really happening. Then she starts to yell and he is completely perplexed as to why she is upset. He hangs up on her.

"American women!" he thinks.

This is also not a joke. I have heard these instances described by too many expat women to count. It is not an isolated incident, but the actual mating ritual of the Spanish male.

Another startling custom (to Americans) in Spain is that normally, the children will live at home with their parents until they get married.

Imagine meeting a nice man in his early thirties. You have seven or eight great dates and you would like to go back to his place. Only his place is a room in his parent's house. Not that big a deal really, since you have your own place. You continue to date and in a

171

year you are married. He moves from his mom's house into an apartment you get together.

His experience of living with a woman so far has been his mother; a woman, who cooks, cleans, does his laundry and sends him off to work with a PB&J in a brown paper sack.

What do you think he expects of you, now that you're living together?

Candy's case is, luckily, quite a bit different. Alfonso has had his own place for years and never pulled the crap described above. That doesn't mean there aren't still difficulties. For instance, Candy sent out RSVP wedding invitations. Then, the week of the wedding, her new Spanish family invited the town to come. Everyone in the grocery store, everyone in the bar, everyone they met on the street that they had known for years. How could they not? This was Spain! No one needed to reply, just show up. Spaniards wouldn't be able to reply in advance. It is not in their nature or their culture. It depends on how they feel that day. There might be rain. There might be a good soccer game on that day. They might be sick. How can you plan things for *the future*. That doesn't even make sense to a Spaniard.

Of course, there is a sit down dinner; at a very nice resort; which is already paid for. To a Spaniard, if the rest of the town shows up for dinner, they'll make it work. To an American, the thought of an additional hundred people showing up for a wedding dinner is a nightmare.

We leave Madrid on Friday afternoon with Kinga driving, Alana riding shotgun and Wendy and I in the back seat. Both these women are counted among our best friends in Spain. Kinga is Polish, speaks three languages, lived in the states for ten years and now lives in Spain doing something involving technology for tele-communications companies.

She drives like a New York taxi driver. Not aggressive, not reckless, but she has a rough time figuring out how to smoothly coast along the road. Coasting is not in her nature. She accelerates to top speed then slams on the brakes when she gets behind a car she can't pass then accelerates to top speed when an opportunity presents itself. This repeats for the entire two hour drive. Wendy and I are flung forward and back as if we are on the least fun amusement park ride ever invented, none of the thrill, all of the nausea.

Sitting next to her is Alana. She is from California and is a major player in "Democrats Abroad" in Spain. Both of them are smart, pretty, single, outspoken and only "sort of" looking for a Spanish man. Having been here for a few years and dated Spanish men, the bloom is off the rose for Spanish romance.

I get a chance to see the south-west Spanish countryside for the first time. For the first forty miles I see what I think is stereotypically Spanish land. A lot of scrubland, a few small buildings, no animals, and a soil color that looks like it would be great for growing rocks and possibly, with lots of fertilizer, a few cacti. About forty miles further on it starts to turn green and then more green as row after row of olive trees appear. More vegetation appears and then we enter another world. It happens the second we turn off the interstate into a different section of Spain called "Leon." Everything turns lush and fertile. Far off in the distance, the gigantic Cantabrian Mountains start to appear, higher than anything I've seen since my parents drove us to see the Grand Canyon, Texas, California, Yellowstone and the Rockies. Wendy explains to me the mountains are what make the area so green and fertile. Laden with water, clouds can't pass the mountain range. They must stay, shedding more and more moisture until they hydrate the land and only then can they rise above the towering cliffs. Because of this, both sides of the road are covered in vineyards, olive trees, cattle, sheep and pigs.

While I gaze at all this in wonder and quietly take notes into my voice recorder, the women are having a different conversation. One of our friends has had a new baby and they named it "Lync." The women are expressing their not very favorable opinion of the name. Finished with my notes, I pipe up with mine.

"I think it's cool. It's different. He'll be unique."

"Oh my God, I'm so not breeding with you" Wendy tells me.

American women....

Like most events in Spain, this is a multi-day event. We arrive at Alfonso's families' house for an American style cookout on Friday. We will not be leaving this wedding until Sunday afternoon. With us, we have brought our very American "Weber" grill for which Wendy had to pay, as the Spanish say "one full eye and a part of the other one" which is the equivalent to the American saying "an arm and a leg." The difference between an American Grill and a Spanish Grill is the cover. American grills have them, Spanish grills do not. *Por Dios*! (By God!) How can you get that good smoky carcinogenic flavor without a lid? Mister Laballe is hard at work on the Spanish grill and when he sees me unloading the Weber his face lights up like a mother welcoming her son home from a war.

He and his wife flew over here for the first time, having never met Alfonso and not speaking a lick of Spanish. He is a typical Louisianan, shirt off, hairy chest, beer belly, colorful shorts, flip flops and tending the grill. He has a spatula in one hand and a beer in the other. He greets us like family, we chat a bit about American grills and I like him already, especially when he quickly offers a beer or sangria and directs us to where they are. He is a great host, even at someone else's house. Inside the garage we are met by Candy's mom and Alfonso's parents with embraces and kisses all around. We grab a beer and then it's into the maelstrom of the party.

I'm guessing there are a hundred people here, many of them American, many of them ex-pats like us, and of course, half a Spanish village. While I am not great in these situations, Wendy shines. She spends her time chatting up friends, making new ones, helping with the party and I spend my time trying to find a dark corner and wait for it all to be over. Franks, beans and hamburgers are served in short order. I am ravenous and devour too much food then head for another beer.

An hour later, time has slowed to a crawl. This is one of the weekends when this little town (pueblo) has a festival. It is described to me as something about burning a bull alive at two a.m. I'm going to need more beer to watch that. We'll be walking into town in thirty minutes to get our spot to watch the burning of the bulls; three of them apparently. I have another beer and check my watch. Twenty-eight minutes to go. I grab another beer, mill about by the pool and try to look inconspicuous and sober. Check my watch. Twenty-five minutes now. Jeezus man!

Finally, it's time to walk into town and we gather up a good crowd to go watch the burning of the bulls. Alfonso's mom is leading. Her family owns an apartment above one of the streets the bull is going to be running down. Great, three flaming, eyes-wide screaming bulls running down the street. Knowing Spaniards, the streets will be packed seven people deep and the festival will be considered a failure unless at least three of them get gored.

Pretty sure this beats Pamplona hands down.

We get to town about 1:45 in the morning. Every light in the place is on. Young children are playing tag in the streets. Teenage boys are skateboarding. Teenage girls are dressed up like they're going to the mall on a Saturday. (Alana says they're dressed up like whores, but I'm being kind.) Adults are sitting at bars or on the fountain sipping a beer chatting and taking it all in.

Everyone is here. Everyone is awake; and I mean everyone. The children, the teenagers and the adults are all acting as if it is July 4th at noon waiting for the parade, except, you realize, it's two a.m.! Imagine seeing a hundred kids playing tag at two in the morning. Imagine a hundred teenagers flirting at romance at two a.m. in America. Imagine every couple and family you know out and about in the middle of town this late in America.

Stunning.

We make our way through the crowd and up to the apartment which has two balconies and wait for the lighting of the bulls.

What actually happens is a man comes into the square in a modified fireman's costume with a huge bull head mounted over his head so he looks like a minotaur. As I imagined, the streets are lined five people deep with some kids in the middle of the street, waiting.

The minotaur is lit on fire. And he starts to run down the street. Fireworks spill from his shoulders. Enormous spinners that bounce off the street, shoot into the air to bounce off a building, then over to the other side of the street to bounce off another building and then spin about on the ground until exploding. Huge sparklers are attached to his shoulders, sending off a steady stream of sparks out to both sides of him as kids run next to him and try not to catch on fire. Then his shoulders start shooting Roman candles into both sides of the crowd. Everyone's laughing and jumping out of the way then taking their place again. I keep waiting for someone to get caught with a Roman candle ball, catch on fire and everyone to point and laugh as he runs down the street, on fire, screaming. All part of the festival! Yay!

These people are insane.

Fireworks continue to shoot out from the front, sides and back of his bull head as he runs up and down the streets of the town. There are kids keeping pace with him, jumping out of the way of fireworks that spin towards their feet, laughing and playing with the burning bull. (Type "Candeleda" into youtube.com and you can see it for yourself.)

It occurs twice more with two other men in the same costume and we have the best seats in the house. Amazing. At three a.m., we head to the hotel and bed.

We get up for breakfast late. Not late for Spaniards though, and breakfast is still laid out waiting to be eaten at eleven in the morning. I'm astonished by the amount of food available to choose from. They have the traditional Spanish toast topped with tomato and sprinkled with olive oil (*pan tomaca*), four different types of cereals, milk, muffins, glazed donuts, chocolate donuts, butter, apricot, honey, peach and raspberry jam, four kinds of juices, blood sausage (*morcilla*), and even *jamon*. Wendy and I seat ourselves with a bunch of her female friends and I notice they're all eating the traditional *pan tomaca*. I'm having Captain Crunch and a couple of chocolate donuts.

I stare out the window and let the sugar high roar through me. The resort we are in is surrounded by gigantic beautiful mountains that are like a hybrid of the French mountains I described earlier, and the Green Mountains of my home state. They are pushed up so far from the bowels of the earth they look snow capped because their peaks are ringed with small clouds. They are covered in lush, green vegetation from base to tip, with jagged peaks and valleys all up the mountain range.

The resort we are in is a hybrid as well. The road to get here is a pitted and gouged dirt track that is beat to shit. I've driven logging roads in the Vermont woods that were easier to navigate. It winds through farms and is probably used mostly by tractors and donkeys. But when you pull into the parking lot of the resort, it looks like a millionaire's paradise. The landscaping is amazing with a lot of beautiful gardens and sitting areas and in the middle of it, a gigantic pool – which is green with algae. There is a man-made small waterfall that feeds a man-made stream stocked with foot-long carp and there are quaint little wooden bridges over the stream - which is choked with debris. Grass, old sticks, huge patches of algae and rotting logs, perhaps put there to make the carp feel more at home and give them a place to hide, I don't know.

Upon entering our room, it's the same. The lock on both sides of the door is a bitch to work, jamming often, and the only way to keep the door closed is to lock it and it takes about a minute to get it open again. If there was a fire in the middle of the night it would be a deathtrap. And yet, all of the plumbing and the room itself looks brand new and shiny. In fact, the shower has a ton of pressure and in the morning I have trouble dragging myself away from its pulsating warmth.

They start to clean the pool in the afternoon and some people go for a swim. Others laze by the pool, taking in sun. Wendy and I walk around to all the cabins chatting with friends from Madrid, seeing how Candy is doing and finally retiring to the front of our cabin to read and sip beer and let other people come visit us. It is a wonderfully social but lazy day.

The wedding starts at five, and it is one of the two typical ways you can get married in Spain. You can get married in a church, or you can have a civil ceremony. In a civil ceremony, an official has to read you the reason for marriage, the laws of marriage in Spain, how it was formed, the duties of both partners, what to do when the marriage goes bad, how to get a divorce, who gets the kids, and on and on and on. The guy drones on with legalities for half an hour and Wendy keeps chuckling and translating for me.

But, it is an outdoor wedding on a beautiful day, the bride looks stunning and the groom can't stop smiling. The ceremony done, everyone gathers near the main building of the resort and waiters pass out drinks and appetizers. Everyone chats for an hour, snaps photos and then we go in to dinner. Dinner lasts a couple hours and then the dancing begins. It is a massive party but by two a.m. I can't keep my eyes open anymore. Candy's plan is to dance until five in the morning then serve morning *churros* (essentially a traditional Spanish breakfast consisting of fried dough logs people dip in their own cups of melted chocolate) to anyone still awake. I'm not going to make it and head to bed, leaving Wendy dancing with the thirty people still awake. She comes to bed at six and I ask her how many made it to *churros?*

"About a dozen of us" and falls into a deep sleep.

We get up at noon and meet Kinga and Alana for the ride back to Madrid on the least fun amusement park ride ever.

I was Promised Kittens

Have I told you I don't eat babies? Because I don't. Let's just get that out there right now, so if you heard otherwise it's not true. Wendy and I went to a wedding this summer and I couldn't eat the kid that was served. And by kid, I mean someone's child. And by someone's child, I guess I really mean suckling goat.

I don't get that. Suckling goat. You know, as in, taken off its mother's teat, bawling, and then killed for my dinner. In my mind, that's a bit different than the food I want to eat. I like to shoot a nice big buck that has had a rich full life banging does for ten years, getting in fights with other bucks and then one moment of carelessness and his full life, becomes my dinner for a couple months. It doesn't bother me killing a grown animal that's experienced sex and fighting and running and all that life has to offer.

But babies?

Once, I shot a spike horned deer and was shocked how small it was. It was just a baby. I felt like I had killed the deer equivalent to a teenager on his skateboard who had never gotten laid, never driven a car, never been in a fight over his girlfriend, never had a sip of beer.

I ate that deer, but honestly, every time I fried up a steak, I remembered how small that animal was. How I had robbed it of a full life and resolved that not only would I never shoot anything less than a fully mature deer, I wouldn't eat kids.

I've stuck to this belief for well on ten years now, but life changes. For one thing, I live in Spain now. Europe eats a lot of babies. They love their suckling young. Kids, lambs, piglets, veal, you name it, they love it tender.

In Wendy's never ending quest to expand my mind, and show me the Spanish countryside, we decided three weeks ago to take a trip to Pedraza with our best friends, Lena and Stefan. It's about ninety minutes from Madrid by car and like most Spanish towns, is built on a hill with a high stone wall surrounding the whole thing to protect it from invaders. Invaders like us who plan on drinking their wine and eating their food. In planning the trip, Lena called us one day and asked if it was okay that we go to Stefan's favorite restaurant. It was no problem if we didn't want to, but this place is usually the reason he visits Pedraza to begin with. As I sit typing, Wendy is talking on the phone.

"All they serve is lamb."

"Oh. I don't know how long this conversation is going to take, but let me ask Jamie."

Wendy explains.

"No problem. I'll eat the lamb."

Shock.

"You will?"

"Sure, my weakly held belief that seems to be changing shouldn't keep the group from enjoying Stefan's favorite meal. No problem at all."

For one thing, my belief in this matter is a philosophical matter, not a spiritual belief. I just don't want to eat babies. Recently some things have come to light that made me not be so rigid in my philosophy.

1. Watching nature shows (from which I take a lot of my philosophy) I started noticing that predators really don't care what age their prey is. The sick, the old, the healthy, the young, they just don't care. If they can catch it, it's dinner.

2. A "Time" magazine article recently let me know that much of the beef I'm eating in the states is much younger than I thought. I've been eating the equivalent of teenagers for years.

3. Anthony Bourdain's commentary: The only people who can afford to make the choice I made, or similar to the one I made, are the people who can *afford* to make that choice. In most developing countries, they don't have vegetarians or people who don't eat babies. They eat what keeps them alive.

Our tall German driver and his tiny Cuban wife pick us up in their four person Smart car. It is a beautiful day, but as we approach Pedraza, it starts to sleet. Then to hail. And then to snow. Real snow too. Visibility diminishing snow. Stefan exclaims "I have been coming here fifteen years and I have never seen it snow; much less snow like this!"

Global Warming my ass.

This continues for the entire day. We drive through the walled gate and park. I'm told it's a beautiful town with a thirteenth century castle, but all I can see in every direction is white. We take shelter in the very definition of a quaint little bar and have some drain cleaner the menu lists as "wine" and wait for the restaurant across the Plaza Mayor to open up. We take seats on a flimsy plank bench close to a big pot-bellied stove to warm up. The room is packed with adults talking and kids playing.

It is snowing even harder when we leave. Making our way across the square I get ready to eat my first taste of baby. I'll just think about the taste and not think of where it came from. I am reminded of one of my favorite Joshie quotes.

Every Friday, we computer technicians from the local high school would go out for Chinese food. I have eaten hot and sour soup in three countries and eight restaurants and the soup in my home town of Middlebury, Vermont is far and above any of the competition. So one day we're eating and I say "This soup is superb. So fucking good. I live for this time of the day on Friday."

Dan said "yeah, but do you want to know what it's made of?"

Joshie replied "I don't care if it's made out of babies."

The restaurant in Pedraza is very rustic. Long tables and long benches like a Norse Viking hall. An enormous fireplace at the far end of the room is roasting lamb. We have some bread, some slightly more palatable wine and badly made Galician soup, then a big platter of baby pieces is set in the middle of the table. Tiny little tail included. Stefan grabs the tail and starts to gnaw.

My first bite of baby tastes a little like pork, a little more gamey but sweet, succulent pork with an aftertaste that lingers. I eat a lot of baby that day because I'm starving and I'm with friends. I still won't order it if I can have something else, but for friends and a good time... sure.

On our next adventure we took the Ave to Toledo. The Ave is cool. A nice comfortable train ride viewing the countryside at 225 kilometers an hour. There are no security checks, no strip searches, no taking off your shoes and emptying your pockets, no annoyingly stupid questions about someone else packing my bag. It is very slick, very comfortable, very modern and of course, there is no turbulence. Lena and Stefan are facing us as we chat and sip wine and no one has to drive. What could be better?

Trains > planes (and even cars.)

In half an hour we're in Toledo which is the tourist-y town I have seen yet in Spain.

Toledo is another small Spanish town built on the top of a hill with a high stone wall and limited openings to get in. It's amazing how the world has changed. Imagine living in a world where you have to have high walls and limited openings for entrance to protect yourself from large bands of men who want to take what you have and rape your women. Insane.

The town itself is pretty, horribly crowded, and everywhere you turn there are shops selling swords and armor, Toledo's specialty. There is mile after mile of shops selling swords and armor and knives and axes. It's a little sad, because parts of this very ancient, historical town now look kitschy and tacky. Stefan and I make our way into a replica store and find fake light sabers, "Icingdeath," "Sting," "Excalibur," and dozens of other swords from literature. Despite the entire store being visible from the register, the owner follows us around, watching us like a hawk. Dude, relax, I am not sticking a sword down my pants; not for love or money and certainly not to steal it.

The things I find most fascinating in these little towns are the Catholic churches. This one was built in 1225 and took two hundred and fifty years to complete. Two hundred and fifty years! Can you imagine?

This church took longer to build than America has been a country.

One of the things that amazes me is the ceilings. Imagine making a multi-arched ceiling a hundred and fifty feet high with blocks of stone heavier than a car – without a crane. The unique feature of this church is the transparency. The church wanted more light inside so it knocked a hole in the side and ceiling of the church. There are paintings and statues all along the side and within the ceiling are angels and cherubs and saints looking in, looking out. All of this is painted and sculpted to look like a tunnel filled with beings and at the top, real sunlight streams in. It is so well done you can't tell what is painted and what is sculpted it blends so effortlessly. At the very top is a figure I assume represents God. If you were to ascend to heaven, this looks like the tunnel you would take. I stare at it for thirty minutes.

"Jamie, go towards the light."

"Not yet; still too much to experience here."

Blown away once again, it is time for some food.

"Lena, you know a good place to eat? You know this town better than any of us."

"Not really, let's just see what we can find."

"Can we have something pulled from its mother's teat and roasted for our enjoyment?"

Laughter.

"Wendy promised me kittens. Can we have kittens today? Or puppies. Either would be good."

A Day in the Life

The alarm goes off at eight. I'm not sure why, since we never get out of bed until nine. I'm just a man, so I don't wonder, ask, or complain. This is one of the many things I learned in my twelve-year marriage. Wendy gets out of bed at nine after nine. She heads to the kitchen to get her morning caffeine, the first of many Diet Cokes. I slumber in bed until the door to the shower shuts.

I roll out of bed, put on sweat pants, a Superman T-shirt and some slipper moccasins I bought for six Euros. I amble down the hall to Wendy's computer and turn it on, then turn on the intern's computer. Then it's back up the hall, strip the pillows off the bed, then make it. I am the bed fairy. The stealth bed maker. The walrus. Goo goo gjoob. Wendy always thinks I'm going to sleep in and then she gets out of the shower and the bed is made and I'm sitting at my desk drinking coffee.

I pour about three ounces of coffee into a cup and drink it cold. As always, I longingly think back to the time when I used to drink fifty ounces a day. Ever since my first massive soul-destroying panic attack, I haven't been able to tolerate caffeine like I used to. I need the three ounces to wake up, but even then I'll get a little jittery in thirty minutes and regret drinking even that much. A pot of coffee lasts me a week or more. Every time I make a new pot, the old filter and coffee is moldy. You can file that under "information you really didn't want or need to know."

I do the dishes in the sink and then check to make sure Wendy's computer has come up alright. Sometimes Outlook gives an error stating, "Outlook failed to start correctly the last time you opened it. Would you like to start Outlook in safe mode?" It happens about once every five times. I've looked up the fix on the net but haven't applied it yet. If it gives that message, the computer hangs until you click "no" and won't finish loading programs in her startup.

I retire to my desk, read new email, then check mixed martial arts sites for new updates. I flame a few people in the forums for claiming Tim Silvia is boring but Lyoto Machida is an elusive artist that only "true" MMA fans can understand. Then I check out my webcomics : "Penny Arcade", "PVP Online", "CTRL-ALT-DEL",

"PBF", "xkcd", then move on to Google news and "The Huffington Post." All of which takes about ten minutes unless there is something compelling on the news or the post.

At ten o'clock, Wendy's new intern Diana arrives. She doesn't know me at all. So far all she's seen is a guy sitting at a desk in sweats, un-showered, unshaved, hair a-tousle sitting in a computer chair as Wendy showed her around the apartment. I let her in and ask her if she needs coffee in the morning. "Oh yes, I'm addicted to coffee."

"Let me make you some fresh coffee then" and she follows me down the hall to the kitchen. Out of her backpack she pulls out both instant coffee and milk. I guess she is addicted. She came prepared. I show her how to use the microwave, where to put the milk and ask if she needs sugar. We make small talk for a bit and I learn about her home town in South America and how much she loved living in Washington D.C. When she finishes making her coffee she heads back down the hall to the other end of the house where Wendy's office is. I'm convinced I've made a good impression and settle back into my desk. A few minutes later the other intern, Sandra, comes in. She speaks English worse than I speak Spanish.

"Hola Jamie."

"Hola Sandra. Como estas?"

"Bien. Y tu?"

"Muy bien.

She makes tea and I want to ask her how her allergies are doing but can't find the right words so early in the morning so I go back to work.

It's very intimidating. At one end of the apartment are three beautiful women, all perfectly made up, in stylish clothes, that have all been to grad school and speak three or more languages, calling some of the most powerful companies in the world. At the other end is an unemployed writer, who went to a state college, speaks one language and is wearing a Superman T-shirt.

Proof there is a God?

Most days at this point I'll do flashcards and Rosetta Stone until my brain is fried, and I need a break, but today I cannot get motivated so I read some MMA forums, some political forums, argue about Scott McClellan's new book and berate myself for not working harder. I am finally able to force myself to do some Rosetta Stone and

"Supermemo" a program that I have put all my hand written Spanish flashcards into over the last week.

I do this until twelve-thirty and then the doorbell rings which Wendy answers. It is a tiny Spanish woman who wants to tell us that barbequing on the terrace is very dangerous and we can't do it anymore. She states this with authority, as if she has some sort of power, which she doesn't. Wendy explains that the firemen had been here before and didn't tell us it was a problem or illegal. The woman insists that it is. She and Wendy argue for a bit because, no, we are not giving up our barbeque until the police or fire department tell us to stop, which they won't. The woman tries to tell us she lives in a three hundred year old house that will go up in flames if a spark hits it. Considering she lives about fifty yards away and a spark's lifetime is about two seconds, I'm not that worried.

She tries to tell Wendy that "as of today, it is forbidden." Which makes me laugh.

I would like to tell her to go smoke a pole, but my Spanish isn't good enough to keep up and Wendy is doing a great job all by herself. I'm sure I'd misunderstand and make things worse so I let it play out. They keep talking for a good twenty minutes and I just keep thinking to myself, "who does this woman think she is? It's not illegal to have a barbeque on a terrace in Madrid. End of discussion. Go away, crazy lady."

Wendy charms her, as is her gift, and they start talking about the woman's dead husband, something about her kid and they part with the woman smilingly insisting that it's forbidden now and Wendy happily promising that we will be very careful when we barbeque. When.

I jump in the shower then head to my Spanish class.

Montse, my instructor, and I talk bullfights for ten minutes and then get down to the dangerous task of learning "*complement directo*" and "*compliment indirecto*" *pronombres*. This is one of the hardest things for me to learn, to listen to, to understand and to use in speech at all, much less use it smoothly.

Pronouns in Spanish work quite differently than in English.

A quick example –

"*Me has escrito una carta?*"

"Have you written a letter to me?" (Even my example sentence is different than we would write it in English. Doing a strict translation of that sentence actually translates to *"To me, have you written a letter?"*

In English, you would respond with "Yes, I have written it to you." "It" replacing "a letter."

To respond using Spanish pronouns, the pronouns go first in the sentence.

"Si, te la he esctrito."

"Yes, to you it I have written."

It's like I have to learn Spanish and Ebonics at the same time.

We drill this and do worksheets for an hour and then it's off to conversation class.

Have I told you how much I hate Italians?

Not all Italians mind you, just the ones from Italy.

Of course, I'm kidding. Mostly. In point of fact, at "International House" Mario "Superman" Washington was from Italy and he basically saved me in that class. I still have a man crush on that guy. File that under "more information you really didn't need, or want, to know." But in general, having Italians in class has been awful for me. Spanish and Italian are so similar, Italian students can speak in a mix of Spanish and Italian and the teacher can understand what they are saying.

Since the two are so similar, and they rarely have to struggle with tense, vocabulary or even how to use pronouns correctly, they speak very fast, so, I can't get a handle on the accent. You know how sometimes you watch movies or TV from England and you can't understand what they're saying because their accent and slang is so different from American English? Italians speaking Spanish doesn't even sound like Spanish to me. So in a class of conversation, when the teacher and the Italian are having a fast paced, spirited discussion about something and you lose the thread of what's going on, you can't contribute. You don't know what's been said, who's on what side or even if they've switched topics. So when the teacher turns to you and asks:

"Jamie, what do you think?"

I can only think - "I think I'm a dumb shit. What do I think about what?" it sort of annoys me.

On top of that, male Italians really like talking and will dominate a class of less accomplished students for a good percentage of the time. So, when you do know what's going on and want to contribute, it's tough to get a word in edgewise.

This week I have a staggering three Italians (the most ever) in the class and it is absolute hell.

Today was entertaining. The topic of the day was fidelity. Raquel was teaching today and while I only understand a little more than half of what she says, it's usually hilarious. She is blunt, rude, not politically correct, and often insulting. She is a little younger than me, nice figure, pretty, long brown hair, hawk-like nose, smiles a lot and persistently hiccups. She has hiccups every day.

She has some great things to say in class today to keep the conversation going.

"Men are all the same and they're all pigs."

"Women cheat less than men because they're more intelligent."

"All men cheat, the ones who say they don't are just better liars."

Unlike the continually rotating students who are only in Madrid for a week or two, I have been in this school for three months. So after each one of these statements she will turn to me and smile because I know she's kidding (I think), and we wait for the conflagration together in silent solidarity, or laughter if we can't keep a straight face.

Spain's not very politically correct yet. Raquel states that "the married office manager that is humping the secretary doesn't love her. It's just sex." At this point, Francesco stands up and adds to the debate something about bending her over the copier and mimes humping someone while standing and slapping his own ass.

The class erupts in laughter, including Raquel. A few minutes later I realize that the class consists of seven men, Raquel and Ula, a small Polish girl who rarely says anything. I wish I had looked over when everyone was laughing to see her reaction. She seems perfectly comfortable in class but that moment would have been telling.

Class finishes and my American friend Tomas asks if I'm up for a glass of wine with him downstairs.

"Yeah, I need a bit of alcohol after that."

Below and next door to the school is the "Paraiso del Jamon" a favorite place of mine. When I had classes in the morning I would go downstairs at the eleven a.m. break and order three eggs over-easy, which is a stereotypical American breakfast and not something you ever see Spaniards do. People would literally walk in off the street, pat me on the shoulder and say "American?" I would chat with the bartenders in my broken Spanish and they would welcome me every morning with "Hola! Como estas Jamie?" I'd ask them about their weekend or how hard they were working and then I'd run out of words. Behind the bar are Reese, Antonio and Maria-cruz. Good people.

Tomas and I order a wine and I start bitching about Italians and the Italian accent and three American girls come in. They don't speak a lick of Spanish and one of them points to the stack of *bocadillos* (Spanish sandwiches, essentially dry sub style bread with *jamon* and nothing else. No garnish, no salt, no mayo, lettuce, nothing) and asks Maria-cruz "Can we have three of those?"

Maria-cruz grabs one and I say "Tres" and the girl who asked repeats "Tres."

"Can we have cheese on those?"

Maria-cruz looks at her blankly.

I go over to the girls and offer some help. Reese comes over to help Maria-cruz.

They tell me what they want and I translate for Reese. "*Quisiera tres bocadillos, todo con queso y uno con tomate, y tambien, tres Coca Colas porfa.*"

(Can I have three sandwiches, all with cheese and one with tomato and also three Coca Colas please.) Porfa is slang for por favor.

I go back to my wine and watch to see if they need more help. In a minute they get their food and start looking for a place to sit. I go back over.

"Do you mind if I explain one more thing to you?"

"No, please."

"In Spain there is a different price for food at a table, food at the bar and food outside at a table in the sun. If you order at the bar it is customary to eat at the bar."

"Is the bar the cheapest place to eat?"

"Yes."

"Thank you again."

"You are welcome."

No more problems arise and Reese hollers across the restaurant "Jamie! *Gracias!*"

"De nada!"

I decline Tomas's offer of another wine, telling him I have a lot of writing to do and head home. I work on "Night, Mare" until seven-thirty, when Wendy finally quits for the day. About this time we'll make something for dinner and watch a bullfight or a movie but she's been cooped up all day in the office, so I propose something else.

"Want to go out for a walk?"

"I'd love that. I need about ten minutes and I'll be ready."

We walk about twenty minutes up to the park where we regularly jog and get a table at a quaint little cafe with umbrellas over the tables to shield us from the brutal sun or when it rains. From here, we get a great view of everyone entering the park. I inherited from my parents a great love of people-watching. We sip a glass of wine and comment on the old folks walking hand and hand into the park, the vast multitudes of dogs and runners streaming in and out and young kids looking for a quiet bush to "make a baby" in.

I love dogs. We chat about the different kinds of dogs, what kinds are the best for kids, which are skittish or barky, the benefits of mutts over purebreds, how Doug is doing, how impressed I am that she picked up all her stuff in New York, shipped it here, set up a life, set up a company and now has contracts with some of the biggest companies in the world. We talk about American politics, my books and running with the bulls.

"Why do you want to run with the bulls this weekend?"

"Well, I'm pretty sure when you get to heaven all your points are added up and I need the points."

"Points?"

"Sure; like, you get a point for each book you've read. You get twenty points for owning a house. You get a hundred points for being a good father and another hundred for being a faithful husband. I think you get like fifty points for running with the bulls. At the end you add them all up and you get to spend them on something, like a house in heaven or maybe the ability to be a rock star in your next life."

"How many points do you get for being paralyzed by doing something stupid and deprive your girlfriend of great sex for the rest of her life? I'm thinking like minus a thousand."

"Um... another wine?"

189

"Sure."

You can tell Spain is not a tip-driven society. While I'm sure he's a very nice guy, our Brazilian waiter has vanished, not checking on us once in the hour we've been here. I go inside and ask him for two more. He asks if I'd like olives with them as the tapas. I tell him that would be great, then I head downstairs to the bathroom. I come out to find him and Wendy in a spirited discussion about America, Spaniards, South American language speaking and talking styles, everything. I can understand most of what he says so we talk for like twenty minutes and I'm actually able to contribute small bits of information.

Wendy and I sit and talk for another hour and then it's too dark to watch people and dogs, so we head down the street towards home and food. We find a nice restaurant half way home and, drawn by the morbid sight of sleek, white suckling pig in the window, peek our head inside. We've had drinks on their terrace before but never eaten here. I order two glasses of wine and sit down at a table while Wendy finds a restroom. One of the guys behind the bar says something to me and I don't hear him so I stand up and approach. He repeats it and I don't understand. I ask him in Spanish to talk more slowly. He does and I'll save you the translating part I indulge in earlier.

"Do you like *jamon*?"

"Yes, very much. I have a *jamonera* (*jamon* holder and carving station) in my apartment. (This never fails to impress *Madrileños* that an American would have and carve his own *jamon*.)

"What kind of *jamon*? *Serrano?*"

Wendy snorts at the suggestion, having just returned from the bathroom. "*Iberico de Bellota*, of course!"

Because, why would you have a *jamonera* for *Serrano?* That's like boiled ham you put on sandwiches. Just buy a package in the supermarket! Clearly he thinks we are gringos.

"Would you like a racionito of *jamon* then?"

A racion of *jamon* is a plateful thinly sliced, just enough to cover the plate. The -*ito* on the end means a small plate. We haven't gotten our tapas yet so I'm assuming that he's offing us a sampler. I have my own *jamon* at home; why would I buy a full racion of the stuff in a restaurant? The stuff is more expensive than lobster!

He starts to talk us up; showing us the hams hanging above the bar and telling us the *jamon* is from a private family business and very good. He gets us menus, chats a bit with us, and gives us cards if we want to buy our next jamon from them. I'm a little leery of this guy. While perfectly nice, he also has that oily used car salesman vibe about him. He finishes his little spiel and then says "I won't bother you anymore."

A few minutes later he brings us a full plate of *jamon*. This is starting to get suspicious. Are we actually being "upsold" for the first time ever in Spain?

He then brings our tapas, a mix of cold potatoes, onions, olives and a light sauce. Then he brings over "chorizo from hell," which is just chorizo sausage in a spicy sauce. He says (which I didn't understand at the time) "Here is the chorizo you ordered." Since I didn't listen to what he said, Wendy has no way of knowing that I didn't order chorizo when she was in the bathroom. When it comes, I just thought it was the typical Spanish custom of "people we like get free shit." (Hell, we've sat and talked with our friend Elvio for five hours and he's brought us a banquet of food, never let our wine glasses go empty and presented us a bill of seven euros at the end of the night.)

Luckily, the *jamon* is amazing. Easily some of the top *jamon* we have ever had. I am sure my next *jamon* is going to come from this place. We talk some more, sip wine and chow down for an hour, then, sated, we ask for the bill.

Not only were we upsold, they're now trying to screw us.

The bill reads –

Racion of *jamon* - 28.00

Bread 1.00

Chorizo from hell 7.00

Wine 4.00

Notice it doesn't say "racionito." Did I mention we got bread? No, that's because we didn't. And notice the chorizo that we didn't order. We did eat some of the chorizo so not a huge deal. And the *jamon* was excellent. Not angry after such a great day, but clearly we have been upsold. And by upsold I mean "screwed." I head to the bathroom and Wendy explains about the bread and chorizo to the waiter. He removes the bread off the bill and leaves the chorizo since we ate some.

I emerge to find Wendy smiling and talking with an old woman who is clearly one of the owners. Now, in many parts of Europe, especially Spain and France, it is a huge deal to admit you are wrong. It almost never happens, even at the cost of business.

Wendy tells the woman what happened, just as information that one of her waiters is trying to screw people, and the woman does the typical Spanish, very not American thing which is to deny everything. It's not important to keep customers; it's important to make sure that the other person knows "it's not my fault, you are wrong."

"Oh, I'm sure there must be a mistake. It must have been an order for another table that got confused with yours." (There were two other tables, both deuces.) "But you ate the chroizo." (Yeah; because in Spain free shit comes all time when the waiter has just spent ten minutes talking to you and you can tell he likes you.) "We've been here thirty-five years and I've raised five kids in this business." (Well, having said that how can we ever think your waiter (probably your son) would upsell us and inflate our bill by twenty plus euros. Because he wouldn't be doing it for more of a tip since tips are 1-3% of the bill here.

But, whatever; we're never coming back and you just lost the sale of a pig leg down the road.

We are in good spirits and laugh about the incident.

Somehow, it is two-thirty in the morning when we get home. We get to sleep around three, rise at nine a.m. and work a full day. I try to take a nap in the middle of day and fail. I do Spanish class, two and half hours working on "Marilyn's Story" and write seven pages of this story.

Thank God it's the weekend now.

Segovia and the Golden Nose

It is November 1st and we are taking a weekend trip to Segovia. We take the train out of the city and again, leaving the city shows nothing but scrubland and then slowly starts to change into more and more vegetation and lush greenery, even this late in the fall. We pass through towns completely enshrouded in trees and then on both sides of the track is farmland and fencing that goes on for miles. Under the trees are small animals the size of deer, antelope or goat. I'm not sure which because they are indistinct on the ground and in the shadows. We pass through some rough cut mountain passes and things are obscured by the landscape, but on the left is the unmistakable hundred-and-fifty **meter** (450 foot) cross rising high above the greenery. It is the *Santa Cruz del Valle de los Caidos* or in English Holy Cross of the Valley of the Fallen, built by General Franco to "honor" those who died in the brutal Civil War where he forced his way to power. He is buried in the main chamber as well as 40,000 other fallen from both sides. I use the word honor in quotes because he used prisoners of war to build the cross over a period of twelve years.

"Yes, this cross is here to honor both sides. Yes, both sides. How magnanimous of me. Now, you on the losing side get to work or we'll whip you bloody."

What an honor.

We check into the beautiful hotel, *"Los Linajes."* Our room looks out over vast swaths of the Spanish countryside. The horizon is covered by beautiful hills with a castle off in the distance. Close by are fields with a tractor plowing, also what appears to be a small Christmas tree farm a short distance away and two small towns on either side of us. Below us is a square monastery with a tower in the center, a small forest of trees made up of what looks like dozens of different species.

When we leave our room we see a sign for *"Mirador"* which means "view point" or "looking place," and we ascend to the top of the roof and there is a platform. We can see to the horizon in all directions. The Spanish countryside is so varied. It is a rocky mix of scrubland, then greenery, cliffs, rocky outcroppings like you would see in the U.S. southwest, large areas of nothing, then farmland, highways and mountains off in the distance.

We leave the hotel to get some tapas and do some exploring. The cobblestone paths (calling them roads or streets would be far too generous) barely have enough room for a car and the sidewalks are half a foot wide. Not that it matters because you don't dare walk when a car is passing you. They inch by while you try to make yourself as flat as possible against the wall. As is typical of Spain, the *Plaza Mayor* is at the top of the hill of the town, so if you're looking for an event, or a place to eat or the cathedral, just keep walking straight up.

We explore for a bit, just soaking in the atmosphere and local culture. We wander up and down random streets, stopping into a couple of different atmospheric places for a chat, a wine and some tapas, then making our way over to view the cathedral from the outside. The first thing you notice is the spires. Immediately I think of Disneyland. The entrance consists of Roman columns supporting a Roman archway, on top of which is a man in robes holding a staff and I know he's a saint of some kind but all I can see is Gandalf shouting "You shall not pass!" Wendy tells me it's actually San Frutos, patron saint of Segovia who, surprisingly, bears a lot in common with Gandalf.

Legend has it that San Frutos went out to meet with attacking Moors and discuss with them the error of their Muslim ways. When they failed to listen and continued to advance on the city, San Frutos drew a line and in the sand and said, "You shall not cross, and if you try, God will prevent you." The first Moor that tried to cross the line cracked the earth asunder and that crack is now called *"Cuchillada de San Frutos"*. The Moors stopped advancing and bothered San Frutos and his followers no more.

"You shall not pass!"

Indeed.

The outside looks pretty amazing I have to admit, but I'm doubtful about the inside. We've seen a lot of cathedrals, what's one more? And while the outside is impressive, we've seen better.

It's getting late so we stop into a last bar, Di Vino, for a drink. Thirty minutes into relaxing at the bar eating tapas, a beautiful woman suddenly appears and starts singing. Not on a stage, no announcement and not stationary, but moving through the crowd as two men play guitars for her. The music seems to move her and she sways as she sings, her voice melodic and moving. She flirts playfully with the men as she sings, leans against walls, opens the door to the front of the bar to sing to people passing by. One of the men passing stops walking and sings back to her in a voice that belongs in an opera. It is amazing. She sings for an hour and it is so moving I want to give her money but there is no collection plate. She has been hired by the owner of the bar, a man known as "The Golden Nose."

He won this title for his skill in sniffing and tasting wine and identifying them in a competition in Seneca Lake, New York. Apparently, he is considered the best sommelier in all of Spain. The walls have newspaper articles about him and above the bar is a golden wine glass with a nose protruding from it.

He owns two restaurants in Segovia and they both tie for first as our favorite in the town. One is upscale, with this late night singer, and the other is Cueva de San Esteban, a smoke-filled rustic Spanish tavern with great food, tons of Segovian townsfolk, few tourists and a tall, beefy lesbian behind the bar. She is curt and surly with me but quickly warms up to Wendy, sits down and wants to practice her English with us. It's quickly apparent that's not all she wants to practice on Wendy. Declining her offer of a backrub, Wendy pulls me from the bar and back to our room.

While the hotel seems new, the plumbing gives hints of being either ancient or just horribly engineered. When you flush, the pipes and plumbing surrounding the room all make a horrible gurgling sound, like the belly of a great hungry beast. And it's not just us; any time anyone flushes the grumbling surrounds us as if we have been devoured. It is so loud the normally deep sleeping Wendy awakes with a start at four a.m. to the great rumbling.

"It's just the pipes sweetheart. Go back to sleep."

We have the hotel breakfast. I love the Spanish way of eating, exemplified by tapas. A little here, a little there, a little of this, a little of that. Breakfast continues that tradition with lots of food in tiny portions. I have a few slices of *jamon*, yogurt, a piece of toast, two pieces of cheese, a taste of cereal, a tiny cup of coffee and some orange juice. And then we're off.

We trudge up the hill to the center of town to see the cathedral. I say trudge, because I am not feeling like doing this today. I want a glass of wine and I want to sit in the sun, have some light food, watch the people walk by and then, if I'm really ambitious, take a nap. But, instead, we are going to walk around the town and see the sights. Oh yeah, another cathedral. Like I haven't seen enough of those yet.

And apparently, I haven't; because as soon as we enter the cool interior of the church, I am once again blown away. These cathedrals are grander than anything Tolkien described. The cathedral was started in 1525 and finally completed, more than two hundred years later, in 1768. And it's easy to see why it took that long to finish. Arched ceilings disappear into the clouds supported by pillars so massive that if ten men stood hand in hand they couldn't encircle them. The outer space of the cathedral is sectioned off into 20x20 feet rooms that each contains a different theme. The first one we enter is like a three dimensional painting. There is an altar in the front, and behind it, a painting thirty feet high. Sculpted around and into the painting are statues, six people wailing and crying over the body of Jesus, to the left of them, a soldier. On the right is another soldier holding a spear, his arm extended. Above that are cherubs and angels looking down, and at the very top, God watching it all. All of it is perfectly melding into and around the painting so the whole diorama looks like everything is emerging from the painting.

Many of the rooms we enter have three dimensional themes as well, but others are like a museum, or an art gallery, containing nothing but paintings that cover the walls all the way to the ceiling. Some of them are gigantic, taking up an entire wall that is thirty or even forty feet high. One of them has a tree in the center with a multitude of people on top of the tree dancing, singing and drinking. Hanging from the tree is a bell. Jesus is next to the bell, poised to ring it. A skeleton with a huge scythe is chopping at the tree and is almost through it. The devil is to the left with a rope tied around the top of the tree ready to pull it down. The message is plain enough. It is judgment hour. It's about eight feet high by six feet wide and dominates the wall it's on. Even the ceiling is painted with suns and stars and angels and everything with gold inlaid. In the center of the room, a statue of Mary, hands clasped in front of her, a halo over her head, standing on a submissive dragon. Everything painted, everything with inlaid gold.

This is amazing to me. I live in the twenty first century and I'm breathless over this. Wendy reminds me that outside are tiny little hovels of houses and imagine the peasants being told about religion in a place like this in the superstitious bad old days and they didn't even have running water, electricity or toilet paper. They had nothing. Nothing. Here is beauty and gold beyond anything they could have ever hoped to imagine. If a priest told them this was a holy place where they had tea and crumpets with God every day at four and instructed them what to tell the others, they would believe him. I would believe him. Today.

This church is a perfect symbol of why Protestants split off from the teachings of the Catholic Church. Was this Jesus' vision? Is this what Jesus preached and died for? The wealth that was poured into this one building to inspire awe in the masses could have helped so many people. I look up and see gigantic stained glass windows sixty feet up. In front of me is another room with a three dimensional picture of Jesus and his disciples made out of black marble and gold. The rooms that ring the inside of the church get more varied and elaborate. There are paintings everywhere. There is a six foot tall Jesus standing in a glass case, posed as if on watch. There are entire rooms dedicated to the Virgin Mary in tasteful blue and sea green. She is surrounded by cherubs and cherub angels are carved into and emerging from the walls, all the way up to the ceiling.

From the cathedral we go to the Alcazar, the large castle at the other end of town, which was the favorite dwelling place of the monarchs of Castile.

I find it much less impressive a structure and recommend seeing the two buildings in reverse order so you can be impressed with both. A few of the rooms are impressive, but nothing grand or awe inspiring. We do end up going up into the tower which has a spiral stair cases wide enough for one thin person and it climbs five hundred steps straight up. Until you have experienced it, you can't imagine the things they allow in Europe that would be closed to the public in America for fear of a lawsuit. I can only imagine how many people have lost their footing and fallen around and down the very steep, very slippery circular hole of death only to stop when enough bodies have choked the tunnel like rats in a sewer grate after a flood.

The steps aren't even full steps. They are tapered triangles about two feet wide narrowing to a fine point in the center of the circle. So the people climbing up have the tiny narrow tips of the triangle to walk on and the people on the outside coming down, have a full, if narrow step. And when I say two feet across, I'm not exaggerating. And this is a very popular attraction. There are fifty to a hundred people ascending at the same time as fifty to a hundred people are descending. It's not just the height that gets to you, it's the space. It's a very, very narrow passageway crammed full of people. If you have claustrophobia and acrophobia, it is a study in overcoming these fears to make it to the top. There are frequent stops as people rest, or get out of the way or just panic and clutch the side of the flimsy chain railing, white with fear and unable to move. Not that I know what that's like, let's just say it was embarrassing.

Of course, the top is worth it all. You have a view for miles of miles of Spanish countryside, Segovia itself, including a marvelous view of the cathedral. We take a few pictures of each other, look all around the top for thirty minutes and then it's time for the hellish descent, which luckily goes smoothly.

We walk back into the center of town and eat at "Narizota" or "Big Nose" in Spanish. In front of us is an eight foot high statue of a man in armor with a sword in one hand and a flag in the other. On each side of him are statues of Sphinx's lying on the ground, each correctly missing a nose.

Luckily, we have this gift of always arriving just before the crowd shows up. It is uncanny. Sometimes we think we are being stalked. We can arrive at any empty restaurant in any town at any time of day and soon after we sit down a mob descends.

Today is no exception. We snag one of many free tables and ten minutes later the place is completely swarmed by barbarian tourist hordes. Our waiter is extremely friendly, fast and busy. Like "The Flash," he is in and out of the kitchen, dodging people, taking orders, filling orders, offering suggestions and smiling the whole time. From him, you would never guess this country doesn't tip more than two or three percent.

Two large ice cold beers in very chilled glasses come, and then we order. Like always, we order what I call the "Spanish pu pu platter;" the typical method of just ordering a bunch of appetizers and sharing them all. The first to arrive is *sopa Castillano* which is a mixture of egg, chorizo, ham and garlic bread in a light tomato and garlic sauce. The one at this restaurant is the best I have ever had. It is heavenly. Second to arrive is a *revuelto* which is the Spanish way of saying scrambled eggs with stuff in it. The stuff today is toasted pine nuts, chorizo and fried onions. I discover I don't like toasted pine nuts. Next comes a plate of *croquettas* which is essentially fried dough filled with a white, slightly doughy sauce and usually *jamon* or *pulpo*. Today, we have ordered one filled with *jamon*, mushroom and egg. It is absolutely delicious; easily the best *croquetta* we have ever had.

Sated, we leave a nice American sized tip for our outstanding waiter and sloth-like, make our way down to the aqueduct. The aqueduct is just a staggering piece of engineering. Legend has it that a woman, sick of hauling water in buckets made a deal with the Devil to bring water into the town. If he could build the aqueduct in one day, he would have her soul. As the day and night wore on, and she saw the Devil was going to succeed the woman repented and prayed to God to save her. In the morning, God made the sun rise a minute early. A rooster crowed, signaling the beginning of the next day and the Devil still had one more stone to place. (So, what the legend is saying is, God isn't above cheating?)

In actuality, it was built by the Romans in about 200 BC.

We make our way down to it and I touch a 2,057-year-old object made from blocks of stone. Then Wendy and I walk around and up as close to the top as we can get. At its highest point it is over a hundred feet tall, constructed of enormous granite blocks. The most amazing thing about this is that there is no mortar or joining of the blocks in any way. The whole thing is like enormous children's building blocks.

We make our way back towards the Plaza Mayor and then down to our hotel for a nap. We awake refreshed and head out to find some tapas. Once again I am stunned by the differences in our cultures. At ten-thirty at night I am sitting outside a little café with dozens of other Spaniards. In the center of the plaza, children are screaming joyfully and playing tag. Young children. There are a dozen kids around the cupola and other small groups of four and five elsewhere throughout. All the parents are in and around the bars and all the kids have gone out to play. In America, most kids of this age would be fast asleep long ago. In Spain, it's like a playground at noon.

Soon, we're back at the hotel and sleeping in the belly of the beast.

In the morning we head out to explore the Knight Templar church outside the city walls.

The city walls stun me.

As an American I can't conceive of what I am seeing. These are fifty foot high walls with two thin entrances into the city on top of a hill. All designed to hold back either advancing hordes of armies or brigands just looking to take your stuff. Looking up, I am once again amazed by how much I didn't know I was missing by not traveling. Nothing on a TV or movie screen can capture the essence of how high these walls are. To think in the movies that men lean ladders against these walls and try to climb over?

Inconceivable.

It is just too high. And you need those walls or people will come and rape your women and pillage your lands. It's amazing to see these walls and the entrances and be reminded how barbaric man's past was and in some cases continues to be.

We make our way down the road out of town and into a park where Wendy can get perfect photos of us with the whole castle on the hill behind us. At the other end of the park is a secluded trail we start to explore. It turns out to go around the outside of the town and is extremely picturesque and relaxing. It winds through a lot of foliage, trees hanging over the path, with cliff faces that start to make up the hill the town is on. There are people jogging, walking dogs or just walking hand in hand like us. It reminds me of the Robert Frost Trail in Vermont, lush and green.

The map our hotel gave us is excellent. We follow the path until we come to another path that leads back up into the town. It is quite a walk. We have essentially done a half circle of the town and I am exhausted and thirsty. We head to Narizota for a beer and some lunch and then it's time to catch the train back to Madrid.

Revelation

I am no longer bored.

I have just finished Ken Grimwood's "Replay" for the fifth time. Well, I think it's the fifth time. When you go years between readings you sort of lose track. Years between readings. Think about the ramifications of that sentence fragment...

People say "Life is short." They are wrong. Life is long, long, long.

Years between readings.

I look back on the different sections of my life, and each one of them has so many experiences packed into them. Each of them is like a four to ten year chapter in the novel that is my life...

There is the high school chapter; the college chapter; the manager of the Middlebury Inn chapter; the computer tech at Computer Alternatives chapter; the trying to be good at Magic chapter; the Marriage chapter; The obsession with MMORPG's chapter; the cancer chapter.

And now there is the Spain and Europe chapter.

All of those chapters were like little lives. Each one of them has so many experiences packed into them; so many memories.

I look back on the college chapter and it seemed to last so long. It seemed to last for a lifetime. And then it was over. And as the years passed and I would get together with friends and we would reminisce about those days and each year we would realize "Do you know that was four years ago? Eight years ago? Fifteen years ago."

Lobsterfest is this fall at my house. My college friends and past lovers will show up with chips, salad, lobster, alcohol and memories. We will reminisce and at one point someone will say "do you know that was nineteen years ago?"

If college was a lifetime, we have lived almost five lifetimes since then.

Which brings me to "Replay."

In the past, every time I read this book it put me into a funk for days, sometimes weeks. It appeals to me so much the idea of going back to college and the ability to make different choices with foreknowledge. I used to long for it. To know my friends in those days of burgeoning wisdom, mounting debt and dwindling funds.

How fun it would have been to guide them both morally and financially. Convince them to pick up some Apple and Microsoft stock. Make us all rich. How nice it would have been to make both the same and different romantic choices as the options arose in the coming years.

How nice it would have been to collect a couple hundred "Black Lotuses" when those cards were selling for a quarter. (They now sell for over two thousand dollars apiece.) Or bet on the Buster Douglas vs. Mike Tyson fight at 40-1 odds and make a fortune.

Oh, to live that life over again. To not make stupid mistakes; to be effortlessly rich; to enjoy that time even more than the first time around.

The book put me into a funk because we only get one life. We only get one college time. One after college time. One set of experiences. And I would read it, and then I would look around and feel like I had blown it. Sure, I had a great life. I had done well by myself. I wasn't homeless living in a ditch. I wasn't drifting between jobs or women.

But this is *life* man! **Life!** The great and beautiful thing! The best thing in the universe and I could have done it so much better! I could have been smarter. I could have made better choices! I could have not said those stupid things at those stupid times and embarrassed myself. I could have…I don't know…so many things.

Don't get me wrong, I always loved my life. I thought I was very lucky. I loved my wife, my home, my job, my lone published book. I always thought I had made some good choices and was in a very good place. But I would finish Replay and I would be filled with a sense of loss; a blue funk like I had screwed up somewhere and couldn't fix it; a deep longing to go back and do things differently. Despite the fact that I loved where I was. And I didn't know why that book always filled me with that longing.

Well, I just finished that book for the fifth time and for the first and only time, I have no deep longing. I have no feeling like I have messed up somewhere and would like to go back and make different choices. There is no blue funk.

And I know it has to do with the Wendy Chapter; the current chapter of this novel that I am living.

I don't know if my meager skills can stress enough the importance of how long we live and how many different ways we can transform ourselves to make the most of that life.

In "The Last Superman Story" by Alan Moore, Myxyzptlk reveals that he is immortal. And immortals get bored. In order to relieve the boredom, he would spend 5000 years exploring an aspect of himself, and then change. And spend 5000 years doing something else. He once spent 5000 years in silence. He spent 5000 years being good. He spent the last 5000 years being a mischievous top hat wearing comical imp. Now he had decided that he was going to spend the next 5000 years being evil.

We do not have immortality. But we have a long, very long time to explore all aspects of ourselves. Life is not short. We are the elves of this world. The only thing that lives longer than us is trees and turtles. (And carp, actually. I just looked it up.)

I've told you before about the way I divide my life into varying chapters. The chapter I am in right now is particularly interesting. At the end of my last chapter, I had never been outside North America, I was married, 213 lbs, short hair, steady almost monotonous job, retirement fund growing every week, house payments made every month, finally bored of Magic, World of Warcraft and constantly wondered "Is this all there is?" I would look at myself in the mirror, see my bloated neck, crooked yellow teeth and I would give that fat alien thing the finger, disgusted with the way I looked.

Today I am leeching away my retirement fund in a desperate bid to fulfill a lifelong dream of being a writer. I weigh 170 lbs, have long hair, a goatee, waist the size it was shortly after college. When I look in the mirror I think with wonder "This is the best I have ever looked in my entire life." I have trained in MMA, competed in a submission grappling tournament, have been to Madrid, Paris, Provence, and Berlin. And I'm learning Spanish. I get up every morning and I cherish the last few moments in bed because I know the rest of the day is going to be "Ready? Go!"

I had no idea my life needed this chapter. I had no idea how to make myself stop saying "Is this all there is?" because I loved my life. I wanted to be interested in games again. I wanted to remain at my job forever. I wanted to keep growing my retirement fund and then retire and Mare and I would just sit at home and read and play video games all day.

That seemed like bliss to me.

My parents go down to Florida every winter and they stay in this little cabin right on the ocean. My brother and sister have both taken their families down to visit and stay in their own little cabin. Marilyn and I were invited every year and we would decline.

"We have to take care of the dogs," we would say.

Wendy and I went this year. I spent time with my brother and his family. It was an amazing time. He has great kids and a lovely wife. We went for an ocean cruise, fished and rode the waves. I woke up and saw a dolphin jump out of the water in the early morning sunshine. There were a dozen manatees floating right off the dock every morning. Close enough to touch. We walked through a nature preserve with alligators.

I did not know I needed that. But I did.

My sister was a waitress at "Rosie's" for, I don't know, fifteen years. It was perfect for her. The customers loved her, she got lots of attention, and the work was relatively easy. And she and I would get together and chat and ask each other "Is this all there is?"

And then she quit.

She got some counseling about why she was sad, got some tests done on her brain and then decided to explore some options. Her counselor told her she needed to do something else. Her road to happiness would start with finding out what she wanted to do.

She took up photography and she had the gift. Some of her stuff was just fantastic. Then she came to work with me as a volunteer computer tech at the high school. I've never seen anyone take to computers as fast as she did. I told her if she kept it up she could get a job at the school with me or at the local computer store. She could be a techie. She worked with me for about three months and decided it wasn't for her. She wanted to work with animals and started volunteering with a veterinary service in Vergennes. I think that lasted a month and then they had a job opening that she applied for. She didn't get it and was devastated.

We could not understand why, but secretly held onto the belief that everything happens for a reason.

Next she saw a job advertised that consisted of caring for forty show dachshunds.

She got it.

Happy happy happy. Still there. Still happy.

Change is good. This is *not* all there is. There is more. There is so much more.

Her husband Todd was head chef and manager at one of the nicest restaurants in town. He had worked his way up the ladder through high school and had been there ever since. He had health insurance and good pay and pretty much hated it and was sick of it after 20 years. Have you ever worked in a service industry?

It drains you. It saps your life. It has a very high burnout rate. Take it from me, I know. I would still dream about working at the Middlebury Inn for years after I had left.

Molly's employer needed a new handyman and groundskeeper. Todd likes working with his hands and he's good at it. He applied and since the "old money' that owns these forty show dogs like Molly so much, they paid him the same as what he was making at his last job so they could work together. I saw them just this weekend.

"You guys still love working with the dogs?"

"Love it," Molly says.

"Best decision I ever made," Todd says. He looks quickly at Molly, "Second best decision."

My friend Steve Savage and his girlfriend Maria sold everything they owned and left a life in Madrid and moved to Australia. They've started up a new company called Cairns Unlimited. There is nothing like a little risk to keep things interesting.

In *Ultra Marathon Man,* a thirty year old executive making a ton of money realizes his life is hollow. His search for meaning arrives when he has an opportunity to cheat on his wife but instead leaves the bar and decides to just run all night long. Now he runs hundred mile marathons and feels at peace. If he was immortal I bet he'd spend 5000 years running.

My friend John is on a ten year plan to buy a boat and sail the ocean picking up work where he can find it. Right now he's taking scuba diving lessons so he can repair the boat in the middle of the ocean if he needs to.

The point of all of this is, of course, we live a long damn time. It is never too late to reinvent yourself and your life. You should never be asking yourself "Is this all there is?" because no, this isn't all there is. There is more. There is a lot more.

John has a stable job and a family. He has discussed it with his wife and kids and they are onboard. He also has a stable job and a retirement fund that is growing every day. It's not going to keep him from living his dream.

Steve Savage traveled the world on pennies.

Ultra Marathon Man got up at four a.m. to pursue his running. He has a stable job, wife, kids and he found meaning on the open road.

If you are perfectly happy where you are - then you can read this conclusion and store it away for the future. I've been there. I have been perfectly happy in my house playing video games and I loved it. I got up every Saturday morning thinking it was Christmas because Marilyn and I were going to play some game for fourteen hours.

I envy you. I'm not saying you need to stop that. What I am saying is, if you are unhappy with yourself or where you are, then change. It is never too late to pursue your dreams. It is never too late to reinvent yourself. It is never too late to try something else. It is never too late to lose weight, start writing, learn a different language, travel the world, sail the seas, and open a new business, whatever!

If you are in an unsatisfying rut, then get out of it.

If you are unhappy- then experiment until you find that which fulfills you.

You do not need a dozen lifetimes to fulfill your dreams.

You need one.

This one.

Make the most of it.

You do not get a Replay.

I hope you enjoyed it.

More of my writings are on my website:

www.JamieWakefield.com

Coming soon will be another book about travels around Europe, adventures in Ecuador, Columbia and the Galapagos, the cancer memoir "Night' Mare" and Quest for the Pro Tour II.

Made in the USA
Lexington, KY
21 April 2010